Secrets *of the*
Coral Reefs

Exploring the
Underwater Wonders

By Rick Sammon

Scientific Advisor: Daphne Gail Fautin,
Biological Sciences, University of Kansas and
Kansas Geological Survey

Forewords by Lloyd Bridges and Jim Fowler

Voyageur Press

Edited by Jane Billinghurst
Cover design by Maria Friedrich
Designed by Andrea Rud and Kathryn Mallien
Printed in China

First hardcover edition

| 95 | 96 | 97 | 98 | 99 | 5 | 4 | 3 | 2 | 1 |

First paperback edition

| 04 | 05 | 06 | 07 | 08 | 5 | 4 | 3 | 2 | 1 |

Library of Congress Cataloging-in-Publication Data
Sammon, Rick
[Rhythm of the reef: a day in the life of the coral reef]
Secrets of the coral reefs: exploring the Underwater wonders / by Rick Sammon. -- 1st softcover ed.
        p. cm.
Previously published as: Rhythm of the Reef. 1995.
Includes bibliographical references and index.
ISBN 0-89658-311-2 (hardcover)
ISBN 0-89658-669-3 (pbk.)
1. Coral reef ecology. 2. Underwater photography. I. Title.
QH541.5.C7S36 1995
57435'2 6367--dc20   957378
                     CIP

Distributed in Canada by Raincoast Books
9050 Shaughnessy Street, Vancouver, B.C. V6P 6E5

Published by Voyageur Press, Inc.
123 North Second Street, P.O. Box 338, Stillwater, MN 55082 U.S.A.
651-430-2210, fax 651-430-2211
books@voyageurpress.com
www.voyageurpress.com

On the frontispiece: Groupers are easy to shoot—with cameras and with spear guns (spear guns, of course, are illegal in marine parks). Coral groupers move slowly and stay close to the reef, where they are camouflaged against the colors and patterns of the corals. Groupers live on many of the world's coral reefs; this colorful subject was photographed off the coast of Durban, South Africa.

On the title pages: Thousands of glassy sweepers, moving in perfect unison, are found in many of the submerged limestone caves along the coast of the Red Sea off Egypt's Sinai Peninsula. With relatively big eyes, sweepers are well adapted for seeing in dark caves and in the shadows of coral overhangs, docks, and piers.

Contents

Seahorse photographed near midnight, Bonaire

Dedication

For my wife, Susan. It's been a great twenty years—above and below the waves.
And for my father, Robert M. Sammon, Sr., who came up with the title for the book, helping me to focus all my ideas.

Acknowledgments

I learned about the rhythm of the reef while diving with marine scientists, many of whom have become good friends. When I was not exploring underwater wonders with these dedicated professionals, I was reading books or attending lectures by other equally talented and knowledgeable people. Without these individuals' years of research and their ability to share what they know in an easy-to-understand, non-assuming manner, this book would not have been possible.

To the following Ph.D.s, I say a big "thank you": Dr. Keith Banister, Dr. Andrew Campbell, Dr. Archie Carr, III, Dr. Jacque Carter, Dr. Eugenie Clark, Dr. Ernie Ernst, Dr. Roger Hanlon, Dr. Robert Johannes, Dr. Robert J. Lavenberg, Dr. Joseph Levine, Dr. Franz Meyer, and Dr. Mary Wicksten. I'd also like to thank John Halas, marine biologist at Florida's Key Largo Marine Sanctuary;

John Forsythe and Paul De Marco at Texas A&M University; and Villamar Godfrey, a local fisherman in Belize.

Jane McHughen, my editor, played a key role in this work by polishing my text, which often was written on my laptop computer on the deck of a dive boat.

Finally, I want to say thank you to a few friends who have helped me with this book, my photographs, my writing, and my personal growth: Mario Arroyo, Steve and Lisa Blount, Stella Covre, Dave and Noreen Downs, Gonzalo and Georgina Gonzalez, Paul Humann, Lou Jones, Emory Kristof, Christine Littlefield, Francisco Marin, Norm Merlis, Sue Pitts, John Rothman, Larry and Pat Stevens—and Dr. John Sarno, who cured my crippling back pain of more than ten years, enabling me to explore the wonders of the underwater world.

Rhythm of the Reef, Fiji Islands
Each and every animal plays an important role in the rhythm of the reef. The removal of just one species can upset the delicate balance of this complex ecosystem.

Foreword by Lloyd Bridges

Since the 1960s—the early days of scuba diving—much has changed for the underwater environment. Oil spills, pollution, global warming, and drift-net and long-line fishing have all adversely changed the natural rhythm of the reef in many parts of the world.

But there is hope. Conserving the underwater environment—and its inhabitants, such as sea turtles, whales, and dolphins—is becoming more important to individuals like yourself, who are encouraging governments to protect natural resources before it is too late.

Most people buy books such as this one to look at the pretty pictures; I urge you to read Rick's text, too. You will learn much about the coral reef ecosystem, from the tiny coral polyps to the large reef predators. You will get a look at the fascinating way the reef changes throughout the day: Like a big city, the reef wakes up as the daytime inhabitants leave their homes and begin their daily lives, while those on the night shift return home to rest throughout the daylight hours. You will also learn why it is important—for everyone—to be a conservationist.

I first met Rick Sammon—along with his wife, sister, and parents—in 1989 at CEDAM International's historic meeting to select the Seven Underwater Wonders of the World. On that day, August 25, Rick had assembled an international panel of experts to select sites that urgently needed to be protected lest they fall the way of the original Seven Wonders of the World and become no more than a sad reminder of what once was.

Rick's panelists, which included scientists, conservationists, and naturalists from National Geographic, the Smithsonian Institution, Wildlife Conservation International, the Aquarium for Wildlife Conservation, and the United Nations Environmental Programme, were filled with enthusiasm for the project; it was an honor for me to meet such dedicated individuals. I announced the Seven Underwater Wonders of the World—Belize Barrier Reef, Deep Ocean Vents, the Galápagos Islands, the Great Barrier Reef, Lake Baikal, the Red Sea, and Palau—at a press conference covered

Lloyd Bridges (right), noted conservationist and actor, accepts CEDAM International's Lifetime Achievement Award on August 25, 1989, from Rick Sammon. Mr. Bridges reminds us: "It's important for everyone to be a conservationist." Photograph © by Robert M. Sammon, Sr.

by CNN and the international press. In one day, we had brought the message of marine conservation to people all over the world.

After the press conference, Rick presented me with CEDAM International's Lifetime Achievement Award for showing millions of people, through my 1960s television series *Sea Hunt*, some of the mysteries and wonders of the underwater world; and for lending my support to various marine conservation organizations though the years, including Whales Alive, Earth Island Institute, Earth Trust, Heal the Bay, and America Ocean Campaign.

I mentioned that I met several members of Rick's family. Like Rick, I am a true family man—something I am proud of. Like Rick, who is concerned about what his three-year-old son, Marco, will find when he goes diving in the next century, I wonder what my grandchildren will find. I can only hope that through the efforts of conservation groups, individuals, and governments, future generations will have an opportunity to see what Rick, I, and my sons Jeff and Beau have been privileged to see.

Lloyd Bridges
Los Angeles, California
1995

Foreword by Jim Fowler

For twenty-three days, the freighter *African Sun* pitched and pushed its way through waves of blue water on a course straight from New York to Capetown. I had not fully understood why ours is known as the "blue planet" until the constant throbbing of the engines stopped. We had finally reached our destination near the bottom of the earth.

When we crossed the equator, King Neptune appeared in all his aquatic finery, and I was appropriately initiated as a member of his domain, as were others who entered the southern oceans for the first time. The experience made me gaze at the stars at night and wonder about the solar system, where I was, and how gravity works. It was strange to wonder if I should feel upside down.

That trip left me in awe of the oceans: their extent, their depth, their power, their beauty, and their mystery. As my knowledge of how oceans work increased—their infinite complexity, the diversity of life they support, the extent and effect of a global network of underwater currents on sea life and the earth climate—I realized how important a healthy marine ecosystem is to the future survival of humankind.

I already know how important the land is to our health and happiness. My father had been a soil scientist. When you consider the devastation that has occurred to much of the earth's surface just in recent times, it's easy to think we've altered everything. But the legendary explorer Lowell Thomas impressed me when he pointed out during a speech at the Explorers Club in 1967 that one-fifth of the earth's land surface was still unexplored. At first, I questioned that fact, but began to realize that when you consider the vast reaches of the Arctic, Antarctic, Amazon, Gobi Desert, and Siberia, he could be right. Since then, I've traveled to many of these wild places, and feel that there is still hope that we can learn to work with nature so that our activities here on earth can become more sustainable—and that some of these wild places will remain wild forever.

That was one of the highlights of my personal quest for discov-

Jim Fowler, author, lecturer, conservationist, and cohost of "Mutual of Omaha's Wild Kingdom." Mr Fowler states: "The key word for the 1990s will probably not be ecology, diversity, or even conservation but sustainability. Sustainability, in fact, is the heartbeat of the universe, the rhythm of life." Photograph © by Brian Janis/ Phototechnik

ery and awareness. Other keys to the understanding of who we are and where we are have come to me since and stand out almost as if they were road signs along the path of life.

I remember when I finally understood that evolution really means that anything still alive here on earth has been successful and has—consciously or unconsciously—continued to adapt to an ever-changing world for its own good.

Then, with the emergence of the terms "ecology" and "ecosystems," the more simplified term "balance of nature" was replaced with the realization that all life on earth is intimately connected and the whole is dependent upon its parts—a system that has been perfected and in place for millions of years. Now, with the aid of tools such as the Hubble Space Telescope, we are confirming what we've suspected: the existence of other planets, black holes of incredible density, and a universe older than we ever guessed. This new knowledge confirms that there is a uniform system operating out there that's governed by universal laws so mind-boggling as to suggest that a cell, deep within our body, represents a physical system in equilibrium not unlike that which exists in outer space.

Another member of the Explorers Club, Dr. Sylvia Earle, renowned underwater argonaut and former chief scientist for NOAA (National Oceanic and Atmospheric Administration), impressed me recently when she stated that the oceans of the world are the last frontier, essentially unknown, and unfortunately not high on our list of priorities or concerns. We apparently don't seem to think that the health of the oceans is as important as the more familiar systems on which we depend. We humans need breathable oxygen, and most of us are therefore more closely connected to the land.

Another member of the Explorers Club, Rick Sammon, impressed me with his knowledge of coral reefs. At the time we met in the early 1980s, I should have known that with a name like Sammon, he was drawn to the sea. My name, Fowler, for example, actually means someone who trains bird of prey; I wasn't aware of just how prophetic that was until I had already worked as a professional trainer of falcons, hawks, and eagles— my life-long interest.

As president of CEDAM International, Rick developed the organization's historic 1989 Seven Underwater Wonders of the World project. I was the chairman of the meeting, and characteristically brought along a young live sea turtle and an alligator who acted as ambassadors for their wild kin.

Many of the places that were chosen for the Seven Underwater Wonders of the World project—spectacular reefs or other aquatic phenomena from around the world—were new to me. Sylvia Earle was right; I thought, "Where are these places?" Rick's subsequent book, *Seven Underwater Wonders of the World*,

is a one-of-a-kind classic; it takes you to these places.

It was at that time that I began to realize that in addition to our compulsive drive to unravel the mysteries of nature through research, we must also learn how to make people care and how to affect the attitude of voters who can, in turn, affect governmental policy so that these places can be saved forever for other generations to experience and enjoy.

Simply put: We need more spokespeople for the natural world.

Stephen Jay Gould, biology writer from Harvard, so aptly stated that it is doubtful that we humans will save anything here on earth unless we prize it or love it deeply. Rick Sammon, with this new book, *Secrets of the Coral Reef*, does just that. Communicating to our fellow human beings our loves and dedication is probably the most challenging task of the 1990s and certainly the next century if we are to slow, and then stop, the destruction of our home, this paradise we call Earth.

I first gathered respect for the beauty of a reef while floating over the shallows in the Florida Keys, then learning how to dive to the white, sandy bottom near Bimini, and finally experiencing the kelp beds of California and the warm waters of the Galápagos. It was a trip to Canouan Island near St. Vincent in the Grenadines with Rick Sammon, however, that opened my eyes to the fact that there's a lot more to the oceans than sharks, whales, fish, and dolphins. To the inexperienced eye, the reefs off Canouan look simply beautiful, from the spectacular lagoon of clear, blue-green water to the crashing waves on the reef crest.

Our goal was to assess the health and size of the reef to determine if it was worthy of being protected as part of a proposed national park. As we dived the shallows of the lagoon, three locals walked from the beach through the waist-deep water and began pulling out a type of sea urchin called a West Indian Sea Egg. Each year in Canouan, these odd animals move in near shore to breed. At that time, they can easily be caught. Considered delicacies, they are sold to area restaurants for a good price. By the time we approached them, each person had gathered a sackful.

Rick had already noticed that the reef was dying; the green of algae had begun to suffocate the coral. Sea urchins are one of the keys to the health of the reef, as they graze on algae as cows do on grass. The coral requires sunlight, and some fish eat the corals, so the whole system breaks down without the sea urchin. You might say one of the rhythms of the reef is broken.

When you begin to realize the everything here on earth operates according to a rhythm, you begin to uncover the key to how nature's biological systems work. We human beings have in the past paid little attention to the fact that we, too, are part of the earth'secosystem and must walk in step with the rhythm. The key word for the 1990s will probably not be *ecology, diversity,* or even *conservation* but rather *sustainability.* Sustainability, in fact, is the heartbeat of the universe, the rhythm of life. Yet if you ask the average person or corporation what the word means in regard to our relationship to nature, they probably could not give you an answer.

Sustainability is a word that automatically suggests human participation and benefit. It implies that a resource will not be available to us if it is not sustainable; that is, not just for the sake of animals, but for we humans, as well. This is a step in the right direction, for as exciting as it is to know about the rhythm of the reef, unless it's clear that its disappearance affects the welfare of humans, we may not see the value of saving it.

Friends, it's the eleventh hour. We may have spent too much time talking about saving the whale and the spotted owl, and not enough time talking about saving wildlife habitat for the sake of humans. Unless we begin to realize that the existence of wildlife and wilderness is desperately important to us economically, spiritually, to our quality of life and to our very survival, we may not save the animals or ourselves.

Rick Sammon's *Secrets of the Coral Reef* is not just a story of a marine environment, it's a story of life on earth. With his stunning photography and powerful writing, Rick Sammon makes people care.

Jim Fowler
New Canaan, Connecticut
February 1995

Manta Ray, Fiji Islands
Manta rays are some of the most graceful animals in the sea. These fish cruise along the reef by flapping their "wings." Sometimes, when they find a good source of plankton, they'll do circular flips again and again in one spot, giving scuba divers a unique underwater acrobatic show. In some countries, mantas are hunted for their meat, which, when cut in round pieces, is sold as scallops. Mantas are also trapped in huge fishing drift nets and on long lines—two methods of fishing that are outlawed in several conservation-minded countries.

Introduction

How can one book—any book—convey the beauty and mystery of one of the most colorful and diverse ecosystems on our planet?

It is with this thought in mind that I begin work on what will be at least a twelve-month commitment. It will require traveling far from home to sites I have not visited before for underwater photographs, going through at least ten thousand of my stock slides to see which ones most vividly illustrate an animal or habitat, and sitting at this computer for hours on end—at home and on location—trying to fill a blank screen with meaningful and entertaining text. So, as I begin this intensive effort, I must ask myself an important question: Does the world really need another book with more pretty pictures of and fascinating facts about the underwater environment? I think it does, and here's why.

Of course, I want you to enjoy looking at my photographs and learning about some of the most colorful, exotic, and mysterious animals on earth. I also want to share with you my experiences— good and bad—of exploring some of the world's most pristine reefs and enthralling, coral-encrusted shipwrecks. The idea behind this book goes beyond that, however. I want to show you the fascinating rhythm of the reef—from the first light of dawn to the mysteries of the midnight sea. On the coral reef, as you will see, there is a changing of the guard throughout the day. Different times present different opportunities, as well as challenges, for all reef inhabitants. The lucky ones survive; the others become meals for predators.

To illustrate the daily rhythm, I've chosen four of my favorite dive sites: the Red Sea off Egypt's Sinai Peninsula at dawn, Truk Lagoon in the Federated States of Micronesia at midday, Cocos Island in the Pacific Ocean far off Costa Rica at dusk, and Bonaire in the Netherlands Antilles at night. Although these sites are thousands of miles apart, most fish, corals, and invertebrates on coral reefs around the world share the same basic rhythm of life. Within this rhythm, each reef has its own signature. Perhaps hard corals or lush soft corals dominate, or maybe there are more large pelagic (open-water) fish than small coral reef fish. Although the coral cities and their inhabitants may change, the basic daily rhythm remains the same. I hope the chapters on these four sites convey the magic

Clownfish and Sea Anemone, Fiji Islands
Sea anemones and clownfish have one of the most interesting symbiotic relationships in the sea. The anemone, with its stinging tentacles, provides protection for the clownfish, which is immune to the anemone's sting. The clownfish, in turn, protects the anemone from fish that like to eat sea anemones. This clownfish was photographed off the Fiji Islands. It is a false skunk anemonefish; the true skunk anemonefish does not have the white vertical bar on its body.

Whale Shark, Galápagos Islands
It's rare to see a whale shark these days because divers, who like to "ride" these docile, school bus–size animals, are frightening them into deeper water. Whale sharks are harmless. With their mouths agape, they strain plankton and small fish from the water. In fifteen years of diving, this is the only whale shark I've seen.

of how the reef looks—and feels—at these different times of day.

I also want to leave you with a basic understanding of the dynamic and fragile ecosystem of the reef. After reading these pages and looking at the photographs, I hope you will develop a greater appreciation for all the reef's inhabitants—from the tiny, thumbnail-sized coral polyp to the giant, school-bus–sized whale shark. After all, how can we love—and help protect—something if we don't appreciate it?

The age-old rhythm of the reef is changing at an alarming rate. This is a story that needs to be told. In the chapter "Changing Rhythm," you will read about what we—relatively recent explorers in the ocean realm—are doing to destroy a habitat that is second only to the tropical rain forest in diversity of species. I would have put this chapter first, but I didn't want to hit you with the bad news before you had an opportunity to see just how magnificent the reefs are today. For now, think about this. Around the world, according

to a United Nations Environmental Programme report entitled *Reefs at Risk*, coral reefs have suffered a dramatic decline in recent years. About 10 percent may already be degraded beyond recovery; another 30 percent are likely to decline seriously within the next twenty years. Some scientists predict that more than two-thirds of the world's reefs may collapse ecologically within the lifetime of our grandchildren—unless we implement effective management of these resources as an urgent priority.

Dr. Ernie Ernst, an advisor to CEDAM International (the organization devoted to Conservation, Education, Diving, Archeology, and Museums) and former director of education at the Aquarium for Wildlife Conservation in New York, knows that overfishing, pollution, and oil spills can affect reefs hundreds of miles away. I have to ask myself: "What will my young son, Marco, see when he goes diving when he's my age?" It is discouraging to realize that he will most likely encounter fewer fish, fewer healthy reefs, and less clean water.

No one book can accurately depict a coral reef in all its beauty and splendor. It is also impossible, in a single volume, to show the many hundreds of species of corals, fish, and invertebrates that make coral reefs among the most biologically diverse ecosystems on our planet. You have to see a reef to believe it. By adding another book to the many fine works already published, I hope to contribute to a greater understanding of why this ecosystem is so important. What I don't want is for this book to become for future generations a catalog of what once was—a scenario that is not utterly impossible at the rate the rhythm of the reef is changing.

For now, I invite you to become an armchair underwater explorer and relive my adventures with me. If you like what you see and read, there is a list in the final chapter of conservation organizations that offer conservation-oriented scuba diving expeditions in which you can participate. By signing up as a team member on one of these expeditions, you will be doing your small—but important—part in preserving coral reefs for future generations.

Sting Ray City,
Cayman Islands
Scuba (self-contained, under-water breathing apparatus) gear enables us to experience the wonders of the undersea world. In only twelve feet (3.6 m) of water off Grand Cayman in the Caribbean's Cayman Islands, divers can have close encounters with dozens of "friendly" sting rays.

15

Chapter 1

Coral Reefs
The Underwater Wonder

In the end, we will conserve only what we love, love only what we understand—and we will understand only what we are taught.
—Spiritual leader Baba Diaum

The conservation organization I head up, CEDAM International (the acronym stands for Conservation, Education, Diving, Arche-
ology, and Museums) has helped set up marine parks in Belize, mapped reefs in St. Kitts, produced reports on fish and inverte-brates for the Bonaire government, developed conservation-oriented guidebooks for the marine parks in Kenya and the Seychelles, recovered shipwreck artifacts for museums in Mexico and Venezuela, and produced slide programs for school children in Palau. These field projects were directed by marine scientists, all of whom have a keen interest in protecting the marine environment for future generations.

In 1989, one of our major endeavors was the selection of Seven Underwater Wonders of the World to promote preserva-tion efforts in underwater environments. A panel of CEDAM International advisors made the selections, using criteria that included conservation value, geological significance, natural beauty, and unique marine life. Five of the seven wonders cho-sen include coral reef ecosystems: the Belize Barrier Reef, Cen-tral America; the Galápagos Islands, Ecuador; the Great Bar-rier Reef, Australia; the Northern Red Sea, Egypt; and Palau, Micronesia. (The other two wonders selected were Lake Baikal, Russia, and deep ocean vents found in many of the world's oceans.) *Secrets of the Coral Reef* is a celebration of coral reef ecosystems and a reminder that our intrusion into the marine environment threatens the existence of coral reefs around the world.

Reef Goldfish, Red Sea
Although the oceans of the world have been given different names, they are all connected. Therefore, changes in the rhythm of the reef on one side of the planet can eventually effect reefs thousands of miles away. The reefs of Ras Muhammad National Park in the Red Sea off Egypt's Sinai Peninsula offers some of the best diving in the world. They are an example of how well a national park designation can work. These reef goldfish are the "trademark" fish of the Red Sea. They hover over coral heads in congregations of dozens—and sometimes even hundreds—of fish.

Why Are Coral Reefs So Special?

Coral reefs have existed for more than 200 million years, making them among the oldest ecosystems on our planet. They are also among the most colorful. Some fish, such as the longnose hawkfish, could only have been created by that consummate artist, Mother Nature; and the magnificent corals of the Indo-Pacific burst with all the colors of the rainbow.

Coral reefs are not only beautiful, they also host an incredible variety of plant and animal life. Indeed, reefs and tropical rain forests are the two most biologically diverse ecosystems on our fragile planet—with species in the tropical rain forest, according to scientists, slightly outnumbering species on the coral reef. In both ecosystems, many species depend on each other for survival. For example, herbivores such as the long-spined sea urchin perform a useful function by eating algae that might otherwise smother the living corals. In some seas, sea urchins are harvested as tasty treats; in others, they have been wiped out by disease. The amount of living coral covering the reefs around Jamaica, for instance, dropped from 50 to 75 percent to under 5 percent after a hurricane in 1980 was followed by a disease that killed most of the long-spined sea urchins. By 1990 there was still no sign of reef recovery. In much the same way, in the tropical rain forest, bats are essential for spreading the seeds of many tropical plants. Dr. Donald Perry, noted tropical rain forest scientist and author, considers bats to be perhaps the most important animals in the rain forest for this very reason. For both coral reefs and tropical rain forests to flourish, we need to protect not only the entire ecosystem but the individual species living in it, as well.

Corals: The Foundation of a Coral Reef

Coral reefs contain two types of corals: hard corals and soft corals. The individual coral polyps are tiny, cylindrical animals with a central mouth through which they eat food and eliminate waste. Around this mouth are tentacles armed with harpoonlike nematocysts that sting and impale plankton and other small animals. On every reef there also are many different types of algae. There is actually more algae than coral on a reef, so a "coral" reef is more properly a coral-algal reef (although that does not sound as enticing to most people). If it were not for the many algae-grazing fish and invertebrates, the soft algae could overgrow the reef. Of the hard algae, two types—*Halimeda* and some red algae—aid in reef construction. *Halimeda* produce calcium carbonate plates that can fill in holes in the reef and help consolidate it; some species of red algae cement the reef pieces together.

Hard corals—brain, boulder, elkhorn, pillar, staghorn, and star, to name but a few—are the main reef builders. Most of these tiny animals, many smaller than your thumbnail, build rock-hard reefs with the help of the microscopic algae growing in their tissue. The coral-algae relationship is a strange one. The coral polyps supply the algae (called zooxanthellae) in their tissue with carbon dioxide. The algae use sunlight to convert the carbon dioxide and water into oxygen and carbohydrates. This is the same process—called photosynthesis—by which green land plants turn carbon dioxide and

water into oxygen and food. The coral polyps then absorb the carbohydrates and, in a process known as calcification, secrete limestone skeletons.

Some scientists suggest that corals get all the food they need from the algae that live in their tissue; others insist that corals are mainly plankton feeders. According to Dr. Richard Chesher, a specialist in systematics and tropical ecology, both are right. Dr. Chesher wrote a book called *Living Corals* with well-known underwater photographer Douglas Faulkner. In it he notes that hard corals do feed on plankton, but not very often and not very efficiently, and that soft corals are better adapted to eating plankton. Because soft corals are true filter feeders, they extend their tentacles throughout the day and night, whereas most hard corals extend their tentacles only at night.

Studies have shown that without zooxanthellae, reef-forming corals do not grow as quickly. On the reef, some corals grow as rapidly as five to ten inches (12.5–25 cm) a year, and most grow at least one inch (2.5 cm) a year. A coral reef grows as hard coral polyps grow outward and upward, most types periodically "hoisting themselves" up and secreting a floor of limestone beneath themselves. The tissue between the polyps thickens the polyp skeletons as the coral grows. Periodically, depending on the geometry of the colony, a

Sea Urchin, Red Sea
Long-spine sea urchins are called the porcupines of the sea. When their barbed spines come in contact with an animal or diver, they break off and are impossible to remove. These animals play an important part in the rhythm of the reef: They graze on algae, which otherwise could smother the corals.

polyp may divide. Because there is tissue continuity from beginning to end of a colony's life, it is almost as if the polyps are immortal. Reefs also expand when hard coral polyps die and other hard coral polyps grow over them.

In late November 1990, while preparing for a CEDAM International expedition to the Great Barrier Reef, I had the opportunity to visit the Australia Institute of Marine Science (AIMS), where I met with its then-director, Joe Baker. From a presentation given by Dr. Baker and his associate Dr. Peter Doherty and from my reading of papers by Paul W. Sammarco, then also at AIMS, I learned how corals reproduce.

Corals have four known modes of asexually reproducing new colonies or individuals, although no species uses all four modes. These modes are: asexual brooded planulae (larvae), which is a type of budding; breakage, when pieces of coral broken off by storms or fish are cemented back onto the reef, where they continue to grow; fission, common in mushroom corals (most of which do not form colonies), when a juvenile coral splits in two; and polyp bail-out, when individual polyps abandon their skeletons and settle elsewhere on the reef to form a new colony. Corals can also reproduce sexually, and fertilization and brooding of the coral larvae can be either internal or external processes.

Five days after Dr. Baker's lecture, on December 5, our dive boat was anchored on a patch reef off Lizard Island on the northern Great Barrier Reef when fellow expeditioner Stella Covre had a once-in-a-lifetime encounter with coral reproduction. "At about 10:30 P.M. I shone my light on the water and wondered what all the pink dots on the surface were. I geared up and entered the water. When I reached the bottom (15 feet/4.5 m), I swam over to a small colony of *Acropora*, one of the branching hard corals. The beam of my light shone like a headlight in a snowstorm—only this time the snow was pink and it was falling upside down. The corals were spawning! I could clearly see the pink eggs leaving the coral, twirling and heading for the surface, like bubbles in a glass of champagne. The 'fizzing' lasted twenty minutes. When I looked up, there was a pink ceiling on the water."

In spring, when the water temperature is right, millions of corals of more than a hundred Great Barrier Reef species release

Above: Damselfish and Hard Coral, Palau
The reef provides many safe hiding places for fish. These reticulated damselfish hover not far from the safety of a club-tip finger coral colony. When danger approaches, they dart—in the blink of an eye—into the deep crevices of this rock-hard shelter.

Left: Staghorn Coral, Great Barrier Reef
Corals and other marine animals have common names, which makes them easier for lay divers to identify. The scientific name of this hard coral is Acropora, *but to scuba divers it's staghorn coral.*

Opposite: Hard Corals, Fiji Islands
Hard corals are the reef builders, and they form massive, rock-hard colonies. This reef has grown to within a few feet of the surface. Corals need lots of sunlight to grow; they can't grow in deep water where sunlight is minimal. Some hard corals can survive for a short period of time out of water at low tide because they have a built-in sun screen that protects them from harmful ultraviolet light.

Above: Daisy Coral, Palau
Daisy coral resembles its topside namesake. Quite understandably, early underwater explorers mistakenly thought corals were plants and not colonies of animals.

Opposite: Soft Coral, Red Sea
Flowerlike in appearance, soft corals add a kaleidoscope of color to the reef. In the Indo-Pacific, red, yellow, orange, purple, and white soft corals are found. Soft coral colors in the Caribbean pale in comparison, coming in shades of green, brown, tan, and sometimes purple.

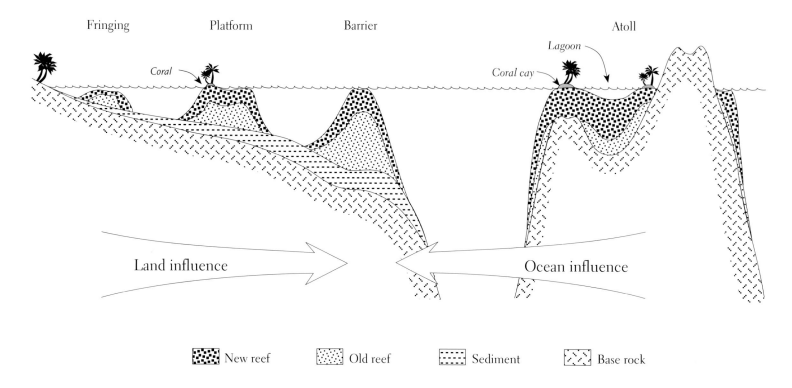

Fringing   Platform   Barrier   Atoll

Lagoon

Coral

Coral cay

Land influence   Ocean influence

New reef   Old reef   Sediment   Base rock

Formation of Reef Types
Fringing reefs, platform reefs, and atolls are the three best known types of coral reefs. Each has its own distinct signature and structure. Platform reefs and coral cays are built on existing reefs over the underlying base rock, which includes volcanic rock and sediments. The major influences are marked as arrows indicating the direction of that influence. Reprinted with permission from Global Climate Change and Coral Reefs: Implications for People and Reefs, published by The World Conservation Union.

bundles of eggs and sperm into the water. When they reach the surface, the eggs are fertilized and develop into larvae, which drift at the mercy of the wind and currents until they find a new portion of the reef on which to settle and grow—if they have not already been devoured by predators.

If hard corals are the reef builders, soft corals are the reef decorators. Hard, reef-building corals have thin, colorless tissue so that sunlight can shine through and reach the zooxanthellae. It is the golden-brown algae living in the animals' tissue that give hard corals their drab color. Some soft coral species do not have zooxanthellae and, instead of clear, colorless tissue, have developed a wonderful array of vibrant colors that adorn the reef. There are, of course, exceptions. Although taxonomically a soft coral, the organ-

pipe coral has a hard red skeleton that helps form the reef, and the hard cup corals in the Caribbean and elsewhere have dazzling colors because they lack zooxanthellae. However, for the most part soft corals are not reef builders and display brighter colors than reef-building hard corals.

Types of Coral Reefs
In the world's oceans, we find three major types of natural coral reefs: fringing reefs, barrier reefs, and atolls. Each has its own distinct structure. We also find artificial reefs created by sunken ships and planes, piers and docks, and oil rigs. Over the past fourteen years, I have had the opportunity to explore all these types of reefs with marine scientists.

Aerial View of Fringing Reefs, Canouan

From the air, the three habitats of ecological communities of shallow tropical oceans are easily seen off Canouan in the Caribbean's Grenadine Islands. On shore, mangrove forests provide a safe nursery for reef fishes. The calm lagoon, dotted with patch reefs and sea grass, is a feeding ground for some nocturnal reef fish. The coral reef is home to hundreds of different species of fish and coral; this rock-hard structure also protects the island from wave damage. Each habitat is important to the survival of the other.

Aerial View of Atoll, Palau

Most atolls form when a tropical island, surrounded by a fringing reef, sinks under its own weight. What remains is an oval-shaped chain of islands that surround a shallow lagoon. Most atolls are found in the Indo-Pacific—such as this atoll off Palau, Micronesia—where there are more volcanic islands than in the Caribbean.

Above: Aerial View of Coral Reefs and Islands, Palau
*Coral reefs teeming with fish and thriving with corals surround the
lush, jungle-covered islands of Palau, Micronesia. From the air, it's
easy to see that Seventy Islands are the tops of formerly submerged
volcanic mountains.*

Right: Artificial Reef, Bonaire
*Artificial reefs begin to form almost as soon as a boat sinks or pilings
are set in place for a dock or pier. The hull of this sunken skiff, in
sixty feet (18 m) of water off the coast of Bonaire in the Netherlands
Antilles, is almost completely covered with corals and algae. Several
species of fish and invertebrates inhabit the skiff, safe from predators.*

Above: Mangroves, Belize
Along the shore, mangroves provide safe nurseries for many reef fish. They also strain silt and sediment runoff before it reaches and smothers the fragile reef. When mangroves are removed to make way for hotels and resorts, it's only a matter of time before the rhythm of the nearby reef changes—forever.

Left: Mangroves, Belize
Many reef fish move to the mangroves to lay their eggs. Between the roots and away from the reef, there are few large predators.

Fringing reefs border the land a relatively short distance from tropical islands and do not include a substantial lagoon area. They are found around many islands in the Caribbean. One of the most prolific and most frequently dived is off Bonaire in the Netherlands Antilles. Here, the coral reef community is easily accessible to scuba divers who don't want to travel far from shore. Put on a tank at the beach, take a five-minute swim, and you're on the reef—which starts at a depth of about twenty feet (6 m) and offers substantial marine life down to about eighty feet (24 m).

As some coral reefs grow older and expand, the near-shore corals cannot compete for food with the outermost corals, which—as shown in the diagram on coral reef formation on page 24—can grow farther and farther seaward, supported on skeletons of their ancestors. A lagoon then develops between the outer reef and the island. This type of reef formation is called a barrier reef. The largest barrier reef in the world is the Great Barrier Reef off Australia. Actually, the Great Barrier Reef is not a single coral reef, but a series of smaller, closely set ribbon reefs that make up one reef ecosystem. In the Caribbean, we find the second-largest barrier reef in the world: the Belize Barrier Reef. This reef runs along the coast of southern Mexico to the southern end of Belize and offers some of the most unspoiled diving in the Caribbean. The Great Barrier Reef and the Belize Barrier Reef (both of which my wife and I have dived) offer a large number of endemic species of marine life—that is, species found nowhere else in the world.

Most atolls are formed when a tropical island surrounded by a fringing reef sinks in the ocean under its own weight due to erosion of the island or shifts in the tectonic plates that make up the earth's crust. What is left is a somewhat circular or oval chain of islands surrounding a lagoon. Land need not sink to form an atoll—sea level can rise. Indeed, 21,000 years ago sea level was four hundred feet (120 m) lower than it is now. Atolls tend to support less marine life than barrier reefs do because the food supply is limited in the sheltered lagoon; however, some, such as Chuuk (formerly Truk) Atoll in the Federated States of Micronesia, offer a host of fish, corals, and invertebrates. On the sunken shipwrecks in the relatively shallow Truk Lagoon (as it is known to divers), soft corals proliferate, and the atoll hosts many species of fish.

Platform reefs (also called patch reefs) and coral cays do not offer the spectacular diving associated with the three major types of coral reefs. They are therefore less known to the general public, even though both are common in the Caribbean and in the Pacific and Indian Oceans. Platform reefs begin to form on submerged mountains or other rock-hard outcrops between the shore and a barrier reef. When the living corals reach the surface, they grow outward—into a platform of sorts—and form a shallow reef flat. Coral cays begin to form when broken coral and sand wash onto reef flats; cays can also form on shallow reefs around atolls. Gradually, the coral skeletons and sand are cemented together and the beachrock, as it is called, breaks the surface to form the cay. Usually these cays, which attract sea birds, crabs, and other marine life, are only a few feet above sea level.

My wife, Susan, and I camped on Ranguana Cay in Belize in 1981. It was about the size of a football field and was dotted with twenty-seven palm trees; a three-foot (0.9-m) wave would have soaked the contents of our tent. We found it difficult to sleep in our tent on stormy nights after the locals told us that in 1968 the cay had been torn in half by a hurricane.

In recent times, coral reefs have developed on artificial structures in the oceans. Artificial reefs provide hiding places and food and attract many corals, invertebrates, and fish. Depending on what the corals are growing on, artificial reefs can become polluted—for example, when a sunken ship leaks oil. Some artificial reefs host just as much marine life as nearby coral reefs. The town pier in Bonaire, Netherlands Antilles, is one such example. Here, on dozens of thirty-foot-high (9-m) pilings, divers can find more corals, fish, and invertebrates than they can photograph in a day of diving. For me, it is the best night dive in the Caribbean.

In the shallow water near a tropical shore, there may be as many as three distinct ecological communities, each dependent on the others for survival. Nearest the shore, we find the all-important mangrove forests. Mangrove trees are the only trees in the world that can live in saltwater year round. Mangrove roots filter silt and sediment that could choke the life out of the corals if they reached the reef. Sponges, sea squirts, bryozoans, and anemones may vie for space among the mangrove roots. If you have an opportunity to snorkel in the mangroves, do it. You will be surprised at the number of juvenile reef fish you see. If you plan to snorkel, make sure you

Bigeye School, Kenya
Bigeyes school for protection from predators, who usually will see the school as one large fish. One bigeye, toward the back of this school, must have narrowly escaped the jaws of a barracuda—evident by the jaw marks on the fish's body.

Scorpionfish, Indonesia
Scorpionfish are lay-in-wait predators: They rest motionlessly on the reef and wait for a smaller fish or invertebrate to swim or walk by. In a single gulp, the scorpion sucks in the unsuspecting prey. Without the aid of artificial light from an underwater strobe, which adds contrast and detail to underwater scenes, this fish is almost invisible to fish and divers, alike.

Multi-Species Congregation, Galápagos Islands
Blue-striped snappers, sailors choice, and a big-scale soldierfish have congregated in this underwater cave. These different species of fish have probably gathered here for protection against reef predators or in search of food. When a congregation of the same species of fish travels together or drifts in unison—again in search of food or for protection—it's called a school.

Above: Caribbean Reef Shark, Bahamas
Sharks have undeservedly bad reputations as man killers. In fact, more people are killed by bees each year than by sharks. Most shark attacks occur when a scuba diver is carrying a speared, bleeding fish.

Left: Sea Lions, Galápagos Islands
Sea lions seem to enjoy performing underwater ballets for scuba divers and snorkelers, coming to within just a few feet of visitors to their realm. As with all wild animals, it's important to remember that sea lions are indeed wild—and the animal might unexpectedly attack if provoked.

spray yourself thoroughly with insect repellent before you venture into the mangroves, or your back will be covered with bites within a few short, painful minutes.

Lagoons and seagrass beds between the shore and the reef are important feeding and breeding areas. Starfish, sea urchins, and conch all feed in seagrass meadows, as do seahorses, anemones, and shrimp. Herbivorous sea cows graze here, and invertebrates such as lobsters and shrimp spend the early part of their lives in the protection of the grasses and mangroves before venturing out onto the reef as adults. Turtles, squid, lobsters, jellyfish, and starfish are also residents of shallow, sandy lagoons. If you snorkel here, you will find an amazing variety of life. Out beyond the lagoon, the coral reef itself is home for thousands of animals: fish, corals, and other invertebrates. The next time you hear the phrase "Save the Reef," you will know that saving the reef involves saving other offshore habitats, too.

Where to Find Reefs

Most coral reef wonderlands are found in the relatively shallow, warm tropical seas between the Tropic of Cancer and the Tropic of Capricorn. Corals thrive in these latitudes because the water is warm and there is plenty of sunlight. Corals like a water temperature between 78 and 80 degrees Fahrenheit (26–27 degrees Celsius), and the algae that live in the corals' tissues need sunlight for photosynthesis.

As with all rules of nature, there are exceptions to coral reef locations. The Gulf Stream brings warm water from the tropics to Florida and Bermuda, and Indo-Pacific currents allow reefs to grow as far north as the southern tip of Japan and as far south as the southern part of the Great Barrier Reef. Some corals even grow in areas such as the Arabian Gulf, where the water temperature is 55°F (13°C) in winter and 100°F (38°C) in summer. These corals are not as colorful as those found in the tropics, but they are true corals that have managed to adapt to temperatures outside the typical coral reef range.

Coral reefs are not found in all tropical waters. Along the west coasts of South America and Africa, for example, cold currents prevent the formation of coral reefs. And even where the water is warm, coral cannot tolerate large amounts of fresh water, which is

why we do not find coral reefs for miles around the estuaries of major rivers such as the Amazon. In addition, the soft substratum near the mouths of rivers discourages the formation of reefs.

In most cases, an atoll begins as a fringing reef around a volcanic island. Because volcanic islands are more common in the Pacific than in the Atlantic, most atolls are found in the Pacific; however, outside the Belize Barrier Reef in the Caribbean, there are three atolls—Glovers Reef, Lighthouse Reef, and Turneffe Island. According to Dr. Franz Meyer, who has led several CEDAM International expeditions, these atolls, unlike those in the Pacific, originated on top of giant fault blocks.

In the Indo-Pacific, there are about ten times as many species of most tropical marine organisms as there are in the Caribbean—for example, ten times as many species of mangrove trees, and ten times as many genera of corals. This is sometimes ascribed to geological history; it is also true, however, that the area of appropriate habitat is about ten times greater in the Indo-Pacific region. This diversity of marine life draws me to the Indo-Pacific and the Red Sea again and again, even though these sites require at least two days travel from the United States in each direction, frustration at airports, and jet lag during and after a trip. The colors simply cannot be matched in the Caribbean, so these dives are well worth the trip.

Rhythm of the Reef

When Susan and I began scuba diving in 1980, most of our dives were in Key Largo, Florida. Like most novice divers, we did mid-morning and mid-afternoon dives, because this is when it is convenient for dive operators to schedule charters. Divers generally show up at eight, the boat leaves at about nine, you are on the reef by ten, you make two dives, and you are back on shore for lunch at one. Afternoon dive boats leave the dock around one, you dive from two to three, and you are back on shore before five. It wasn't until we began our live-aboard diving adventures that we could really explore the reef around the clock. Once we started making these dives, I was up before sunrise and always first in the water. I now dive as often as five times a day, from sunrise to after sunset.

In the beginning, the sights we saw under water were overwhelming, and I photographed everything in sight without really

Sleeping Turtle, South Africa
Hawksbill turtles are identified by their hawklike mouths. During the day, these animals cruise the reef and open water in search of food, usually jellyfish. At night, they rest under rock ledges so they don't float to the surface, where they could become prey for sharks.

Above: Guineafowl Puffer in Yellow Phase, Cocos Island
In its yellow phase, the guineafowl puffer stands out on the reef like a beacon, perhaps making the fish attractive to a mate. Photograph © by Stella Covre

Right: Guineafowl Puffer in Spotted Phase, Cocos Island
Many fish change color throughout the day, making identification difficult for the novice diver. The guineafowl puffer, for example, has two phases: a yellow phase and a spotted phase. While it's changing color, there's also an in-between period. In its spotted phase, the guineafowl puffer is well camouflaged (in natural light) against the reef.

Above: Hawkfish in Red Camouflage, Fiji Islands
These longnose hawkfish have changed color to blend in with the sea fans on which they rest.

Left: Hawkfish in Pale Camouflage, Red Sea
The longnose hawkfish can change color to match its surroundings. This solitary hawkfish rests on a sea fan at night.

Sweeper School at Dawn, Red Sea

During daylight hours, the sight of hundreds of sweepers hovering over a Red Sea coral head is not uncommon. At night, however, these fish tuck safely inside the nooks and crannies of the reef.

Clownfish, Fiji Islands
These two-bar clownfish are hiding in the protective tentacles of a sea anemone.

Barberfish in Daytime Phase, Cocos Island
During the day the barberfish is bright yellow.

Barberfish in Nighttime Phase, Cocos Island
At night the barberfish pales to a silvery-white, and blends in with the white sand, helping the fish avoid detection by predators. The lateral line—an organ on the side of the fish's body that helps it detect movement in the surrounding water—is easily seen in both phases.

understanding what was going on. As I became more experienced and started diving with marine scientists who have dedicated their lives to coral reef conservation and marine science, I began to learn how the reef and its inhabitants change throughout the cycle of the day.

Dawn is the wake-up call on the reef, with sunlight triggering responses in diurnal fish—including angelfish, hawkfish, trumpetfish, and wrasses—to begin feeding and, in certain species, spawning. As the diurnal fish leave the safety of the nooks and crannies of the reef, the nocturnal fish—bigeyes, sweepers, eels, and snappers, to name a few—return from a night of feeding on the reef and in the nearby seagrass beds to their familiar daytime hiding places, avoiding the hassle of having to seek out a new shelter every day. This is a time of intense activity on the reef, and I have taken some of my best pictures during these hours.

Many daytime species—including convictfish, bluetangs, and surgeonfish—form squads and hunt in daily migrations over the reef. Angelfish and butterflyfish (which usually mate for life) hunt in pairs. There are also solitary hunters and feeders, such as trumpetfish, trunkfish, pufferfish, and fairy basslets. Then there are species, such as clownfish, blennies, and gobies, that never stray far from home.

At midday, things are usually pretty quiet on the reef—except when an opportunistic feeder, such as a shark, eel, grouper, jack, barracuda, or lizardfish, encounters a smaller fish. These reef predators usually feed at dawn or dusk but will also feed during the day if the opportunity presents itself.

Things pick up again around dusk as the diurnal fish return home and the nocturnal feeders start their shift. Under the cover of darkness, the nocturnal fish and invertebrates begin their hunt for food—and the struggle for survival. Some reef fish, such as hogfish and three-banded butterflyfish, lose their bright poster colors and turn pale to blend in with the sand on which they sleep; other fish, including many wrasses, actually bury themselves in the sand to avoid detection by nocturnal predators.

Not only are there different fish and invertebrates to see during the different hours of the day, but the quality of light on the reef makes each dive different almost from hour to hour. From mid-morning to mid-afternoon, it is brightest under water, which is ideal for taking panoramic shots of the reef and for photographing its inhabitants in natural light. Before and after these hours, sunlight penetrates the water at an angle, creating dramatic shafts of light that shimmer in clear water. At dawn and dusk, light is subdued; after dark, as you explore the reef, you feel you are moving down a road on a moonless night seeing only what is in the beam of your flashlight.

To take photographs under water, you need an understanding not only of the basic rules of photography but also of how these rules change in an underwater environment. Water, which is eight hundred times denser than air, filters out colors selectively as depth increases and refracts light to make subjects appear closer than they actually are; different times of day call for different techniques and equipment. During the day and at dawn and dusk, I generally do wide-angle photography with a Nikonos V camera and a 15mm or 20mm lens; I also use an SLR in a housing with a wide-angle zoom lens. When taking natural-light pictures, I use either Underwater Ektachrome film, designed specifically for underwater shooting, or I use a color correction filter, which adds some color back into shallow reef scenes, to a depth of about forty feet (12 m).

The deeper you dive, the more colors you lose. The red component of light goes first. In clear water red is completely filtered out at approximately fifteen feet (4.5 m). Orange is completely filtered out at about eighteen feet (5.4 m); yellow goes at forty-five feet (13.5 m). For images that burst with color, I shoot with a dual strobe that lights the scene artificially. To compensate for refraction and to capture as much natural color as possible, I get as close to my subjects as I can. At night, I almost always shoot close-ups of fish (because they are sleeping and are easy to photograph), corals, and other invertebrates with a 35mm AF SLR/macro lens setup in an underwater housing with dual strobes.

If you want pictures that tell the whole story of your dive vacation from dawn to after dusk, I recommend paying heed to the expression "If you snooze, you lose." Get up early, have a cup of coffee, and be the first in the water. You'll see sights most divers miss. I recommend taking a nap in the afternoon so you will have energy to make a night dive.

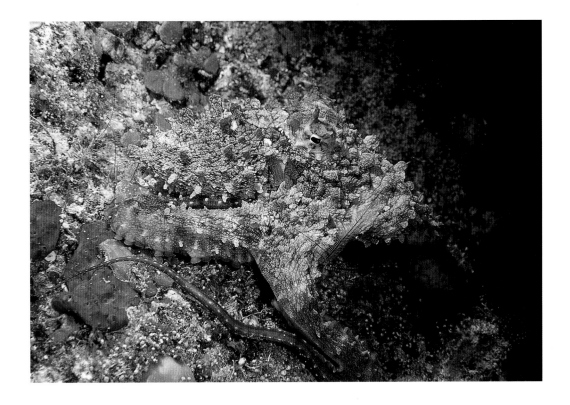

Octopus Camouflage, Fiji Islands
The octopus is a master of camouflage. In the blink of an eye, it can change its color, shape, and even body texture to perfectly match its surroundings—making it invisible to predators and prey. This octopus was photographed on a night dive.

Octopus Camouflage, Fiji Islands
Within a single minute, the same octopus has changed its coloring, and in its camouflaged state it is virtually impossible to see. When swimming, it's more easily detected.

Chapter 2

Sunrise on the Reef

The Red Sea, Egypt

From the aft deck of the *Colona IV*, I watch a fiery yellow ball slowly rise from the distant horizon, lighting the cloudless sky and illuminating the deep blue, calm sea. Ever so slowly, the scene gets brighter and brighter—so bright that I need my sunglasses, even though it is only just past six in the morning.

I follow the graceful flight of a lone brown booby toward the bow, and the bleak and barren tip of the Sinai Peninsula—where the Gulf of Aqaba and the Gulf of Suez meet—comes into faint view. Rising almost one hundred feet (30 m) from the desert, the rocky bluff of Ras Muhammad (the head, or cape, of Muhammad) seems to solemnly watch the dawn of a new day. Two hundred thousand years ago, Ras Muhammad was a living coral reef, submerged in the nutrient-rich waters of the Red Sea. Today, it is a solid block of fossilized coral, with the imprints of hard corals easily distinguishable in the limestone walls surrounding the bluff.

As I sip a cup of lukewarm instant coffee—one of the hardships of diving from live-aboard boats—I realize this is the fifteenth sunrise I've seen on the Red Sea and the beginning of my third major week-long exploration of this site. I am here with eight other CEDAM International divers to identify and document the anemones and anemonefish in the area. The director of the expedition is invertebrate zoologist Dr. Daphne Fautin of the University of Kansas, who recently co-wrote the best-selling book *A Field Guide to Anemonefishes and their Host Sea Anemones* with Gerald R. Allen.

The Red Sea is considered one of the Seven Underwater Wonders of the World by marine scientists, conservationists, and scuba divers. It is the Red Sea's diversity of marine life that has earned it the coveted title of Underwater Wonder. Dr. John Randall, noted marine scientist and author, suggests that there are at least one thousand species of tropical fish living here, with names like Napoleon fish, peacock rock cod, fringed porcupine fish, and sergeant major, and that 17 percent of these are endemic. Coral experts also are awed by the variety of species. They estimate that here there are

Reef Goldfish, Red Sea
With its brilliantly colored corals, exotic fish, and year-round warm and sunny weather, the Red Sea attracts divers from around the world. At daybreak on this small section of Alternatives Reef, hundreds of reef goldfish flutter about, picking out plankton from the water. This non-stop action takes place against a background of colorful hard and soft corals.

Above: Fossilized Coral Reef, Red Sea
Two hundred thousand years ago, Ras Muhammad, or the "head of Muhammad," was a thriving coral reef. Today, it is a block of fossilized coral. The limestone ledge in the foreground is only a few inches under water. Below, dozens of fish-filled caves offer unique scuba diving experiences.

Right: Sinai Desert Bordering the Red Sea
The land surrounding the Red Sea is a bleak, barren, and almost colorless desert, supporting relatively little life. Under water, the scene is quite different. Scientists estimate that one thousand species live in the Red Sea, and that 17 percent of these are endemic.

Dawn on the Reef, Red Sea
Wherever I go diving, I make it a point to get up early and make a dive before breakfast. During first light, the reef is a magical place, filled with beauty, wonder, and a quality of light that is almost indescribable. Still, you need artificial light to see the true colors of the reef. The bright red and orange soft corals in the foreground look dark brown in natural light.

43

four hundred species of hard and soft corals, which depend on sunlight to grow — in one of the year-round sunniest places on earth.

To find the answer to this incredible diversity of marine life, we need to go back in time. Thirty million years ago, the south end of the Red Sea did not open to the Indian Ocean as it does today, and the sea was connected instead to the Mediterranean Sea at the north. At that time, the Red Sea served as a breeding ground for fish and corals of the Atlantic. Ten million years later, as tectonic plates shifted, the northern straits closed and new straits opened to the south. The resulting sea includes flora and fauna of both the Atlantic and Indian Oceans, with Indo-Pacific species predominating.

From a non-scientific point of view, the Red Sea offers scuba divers a visual treat of colorful and exotic fish and corals, endless photo opportunities, and the thrill of floating in unusually clear water like astronauts in space. What is more, it almost never rains here. The cloud-free sky and the predictable weather make the topside experience of traveling from site to site a peaceful and enjoyable one.

I'm excited about my renewed exploration of the Red Sea and begin to gear up for the dawn dive with my dive buddy, Daphne. The assignment we have given ourselves today is to document the anemones and clownfish of a site called Anemone City, a section of the reef that is home to dozens of these photogenic animals and the playful anemonefish that make their homes among the anemones' tentacles.

We want to get in the water soon, for during the hour or so of crepuscular light at the beginning and the end of each day, divers have an opportunity to see the greatest number of fish on the reef. Nocturnal fish such as squirrelfish, bigeyes, and snappers are heading home to the nooks and crannies of the reef after a night of feeding, while diurnal angelfish, triggerfish, and butterflyfish that, perhaps due to limited space, share hiding places in the reef with the nighttime feeders, are waking up and beginning their search for food. During this changing of the guard, piscivores — fish-eaters such as sharks, barracudas, groupers, and jacks — are on patrol. Small prey fish know this and they are skittish. But as I ready my three cameras and Daphne checks her underwater writing slates, we know that we will be lucky if we see a fish eat a fish, as a predatory snap of the jaws happens in a heartbeat.

About twelve hours from now, at dusk, we will have another opportunity to make a dive in the half light, when the scenario of nocturnal and diurnal fish is reversed. Daphne and I agree, however, that there is something very special about dawn dives. It has to do with the way the light bathes the reef, softening shadows and reducing contrast — in the same way an overcast sky softens landscape and seascape scenes; and the way the water surrounding a diver looks from below at dawn — when there is no visible distinction between the water column and surface as there is when the sun is overhead.

We leap off the dive deck into a new world filled with dazzling visual wonders. Under water, the encircling cloud of bubbles caused by our entry rapidly clears. We are hovering effortlessly in blue space. Visibility is perhaps two hundred feet (60 m), a rare treat for

scuba divers. Even though the water is clear, at a depth of forty feet (12 m) the water between us and the surface has dulled the colors of the reef, making it appear pale blue. To compensate for the color-loss property of water, I turn on my dive light to bring out the true colors of the fish and corals as I approach the reef. I also activate my cameras' flash units, essential for capturing the reef's dramatic colors on film.

As we near the gently sloping reef, the scene becomes a chaotic jumble of intricate coral formations in a kaleidoscope of colors. The soft corals look like delicate, flowering plants in shades of red, purple, white, orange, and yellow; the hard corals, the reef builders, create bizarre brown, tan, yellow, and green coral castles. Added to the chaos are many hundreds of oddly shaped exotic fish, painted by nature with colors, lines, and patterns that make them some of the most beautiful creatures on earth. My job as a photographer is to isolate subjects from the wild array of shapes and colors—to make some sense of the overwhelming scene so viewers can appreciate the beauty of the individual reef inhabitants.

About five minutes into our dive, Daphne and I spot three anemones, with several two-banded clownfish hovering overhead.

Sergeant Majors, Red Sea
Near Ras Muhammad the reef begins just a few inches below the surface, giving snorkelers a look at the intricate and colorful world of the coral reef ecosystem. Here, sergeant majors are guarding their eggs, laid among the hard corals within the past day or two.

Theirs is one of the most interesting—and definitely one of the most photographed—symbiotic relationships in the sea. The anemone, an animal that attaches itself to the reef, has stinging tentacles to trap small fish, shrimp, and other animals for food and to ward off any reef fish looking for a tasty tentacle treat. For added protection, the anemone has at least one pair of resident clownfish guards, which the anemone does not sting. When an anemone predator, such as a butterflyfish, approaches, the clownfish dart out, pecking at a fin or scale, and in most cases forcing the fish to seek an easier meal. For the clownfish, the anemone provides protection from reef patrollers that like to eat small fish but do not like to get stung in the process. At the first sign of danger, the clownfish dart into the protective tentacles, where they hide until the danger has passed.

Before we started our dive this morning, Daphne filled me in on the sex life of anemonefish. "Basically," she said, "clownfish are hermaphrodites. They have male and female sex organs, though not both at the same time. The advantage to being hermaphrodites is that the species has a great chance of reproducing—and survival. A typical anemone hosts an adult male and an adult female anemonefish and a few juveniles. If the female is eaten or dies, the adult male makes a quick change into a breeding female, and the largest juvenile turns into a breeding male." I look at the clownfish in a different light as I make a few exposures before moving on.

As we continue our early morning exploration of Ras Muhammad, I photograph the beautiful and graceful butterflyfish that flutter around the coral heads like butterflies around flowers. Butterflyfish—like many other diurnal fish—shy away from divers during the day. At this time in the morning, they are still groggy from a good night's sleep, so I approach them seemingly unnoticed. First I capture on film the bluecheek butterflyfish, a bright yellow fish with a splash of blue on its cheeks. Then, the raccoon butterflyfish, with its raccoonlike face mask, comes into focus. I have seen and photographed many butterflyfish in the Caribbean, but none as colorful as these two species.

Butterflyfish, like other free-swimming fish, have an amazing device that helps them maintain neutral buoyancy: a gas bladder, also called a swim bladder. According to noted naturalists Roberta

Above: Anemone City, Red Sea
Near Ras Muhammad is so-called Anemone City, home for dozens of sea anemones and their resident two-bar clownfish. The anemone, an animal that attaches itself to the reef, has tentacles that can sting and trap most reef fish. "The clownfish is immune to the anemone's sting. For its share in this symbiotic relationship, the clownfish drives away the few fish that do eat anemone tentacles.

Right: Anemone and Clownfish, Red Sea
A typical anemone hosts adult male and adult female two-bar clownfish and a few juveniles. The tiny, dotted dominofish are commonly found swimming around anemones, but they stay far away from the animal's stinging tentacles.

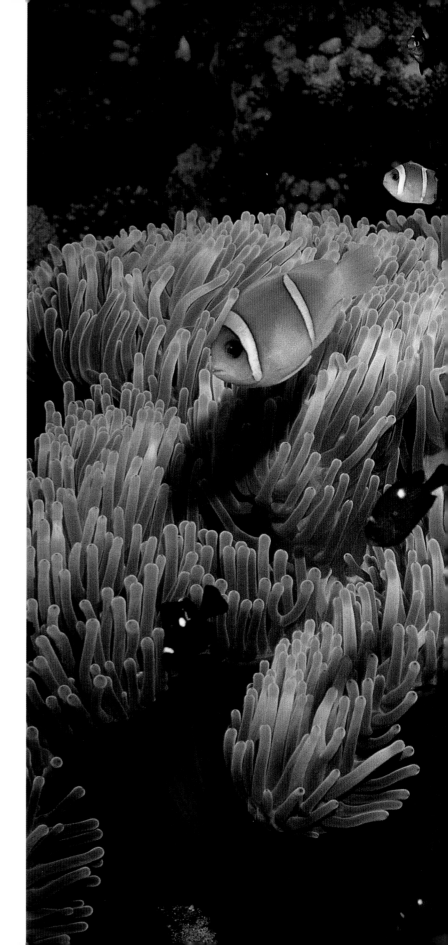

Anemone City, Red Sea
Not all anemones in the Red Sea have such dramatically colored red bases, which, without the aid of artificial light, look dark brown at a depth of forty-five feet (13.5 m). This photograph shows three individual anemones. Surrounding the anemone are dozens of dominofish, which are commonly found around anemones.

Clownfish, Red Sea
Adult two-bar clownfish are approximately two inches (5 cm) long. But even at this small size, they will dart out from within the anemone's protective tentacles to attack potential predators many times their size. They also nip scuba divers and attack their own reflections in a diver's mask.

and James Wilson, authors of the Pisces guide *Watching Fishes*, "[Fish] inflate their bladders with air extracted from the water by their gills and carried to the bladder through a complex array of capillaries. To deflate, they re-absorb excess air back into the bloodstream." Scuba divers maintain neutral buoyancy in a similar manner. They wear a B.C. (buoyancy compensator) vest that can be inflated with air from the scuba tank and deflated through a vent, making them weightless. There are species of fish that do not have a gas bladder. Many of these make their home on the reef and sandy bottom of the lagoon. These fish, called bottom dwellers, are usually "lie-in-wait" predators that use camouflage to hide from other predators and to avoid detection by potential prey.

On our dive, Daphne and I encounter several of these bottom dwellers. First we see a lionfish (also called firefish, zebrafish, or turkeyfish) with dorsal fins that can inflict a painful sting on another fish or on a scuba diver. The ever-so-slow–moving lionfish uses these fins to herd smaller fish into nooks in the reef. Once cornered, the lionfish sucks the small fish into its mouth in a single gulp.

Moving along, we spot several species of hawkfish: longnose, freckleface, and red-spotted. A hawkfish uses its ventral (pelvic) fins to perch on a coral ledge and wait for a small fish to swim by, much the way a hawk perches on a branch. In the blink of an eye, the hawkfish sucks the smaller fish into its mouth, and the predator returns to its resting spot to wait patiently for the next meal to come by.

Other bottom dwellers we encounter are the lizardfish, which has a body shaped like a lizard, and the crocodilefish, which has a crocodilelike snout. I am grateful for the common names given to reef creatures, for the scientific names are too hard for me to remember. Besides, crocodilefish sounds more interesting, to most people anyway, than *Platycephalus tuberculatus*.

We are getting low on air and need to begin our ascent to the surface. As we glide over the reef crest, just a few feet below the surface, I notice a pile of small, broken crab shells piled neatly on the reef. Having dived with octopus experts Dr. Roger Hanlon and John Forsythe in Tahiti and in Little Cayman, I know these shells mark the den of an octopus, which discards the shells after dining

on the animals within.

Taking a close look, I'm surprised to see an octopus staring back at me. Usually octopuses hide deep within the reef. I'm even more surprised to see the octopus first poke its head out of the den and then begin a reef walk toward the deep water. Daphne and I follow this reef creature as it changes body color and texture to match its surroundings. So much for the theory that octopuses are strictly nocturnal animals.

According to Dr. Keith Banister and Dr. Andrew Campbell, who recently published the *Encyclopedia of Aquatic Life*, the octopus changes color by means of pigment cells in the skin called chromatophores. When muscles that radiate from the edge of the chromatophores contract, the pigment in the cells is concentrated, and the animal becomes darker. When they relax, the opposite occurs. These muscles are under the control of the octopus's nervous system and have been the subject of considerable research. Indeed, studies of the nervous system and the brain of the octopus have led to a better understanding of how the human nervous system functions.

As we make our way back to the *Colona IV*, we fly through a cloud of reef goldfish, also known as lyretail coralfish. These fish are in constant motion, picking out near-microscopic plankton from the water and darting back into the safety of the reef, in unison, when a predator approaches. I make my last exposure on these trademark fish of the Red Sea and head toward the surface.

Once again, the Red Sea has provided me with visual treats and one-of-a-kind photo opportunities—and, I hope, photographs that capture the beauty of this underwater wonderland. Now it is almost seven thirty and time for breakfast. In an hour, I'll be back in the water, making the second of my four or five dives today.

* * *

It is six in the morning on the second day of my expedition to the Red Sea. Once again, I'm first on deck, eager to be first in the water. Today I want to dive alone and work on a single picture that will capture the beauty and drama of the many caves around Ras Muhammad. For a photographer, diving alone has several advantages. There are fewer air bubbles from scuba tanks and therefore less noise to scare the fish; there is no chance of having another diver's fin show up in the corner of a picture; and there is no one to kick up silt and sediment from the reef, which can ruin a picture. To top it all, there is a feeling of solitude that, for many divers, comes close to a mystical experience. I am well aware that dive training organizations strongly recommend diving with a buddy, so I will be extra cautious and not take any chances.

Captain Freddy Storheil, our Norwegian skipper, has dropped me at site called Fishermen's Bank, a near-vertical underwater wall of coral. Visibility is again about two hundred feet (60 m). It doesn't take me long to spot the cave Freddy mentioned during his thorough briefing on deck. Turning on the dive light mounted on my camera, I slowly proceed into the darkness.

Inside the cave I'm surrounded by a swarm of inch-long (2.5-cm) glassy sweepers with copper bodies. As they dart in unison around the cave, the fluttering of their fins reminds me of the sound of a flock of Canada geese flying overhead back in upstate New York. Turning around and looking out toward the blue sea, I see bold shafts of light penetrating small openings in the roof of the cave. They add an ethereal look to the scene, and I'm reminded of what my good friend and diving buddy Dr. Larry Stevens says about an underwater experience like this: "It's better than church."

I have to shoot fast, because the bubbles from my regulator are hitting the ceiling of the cave, causing a sediment snowstorm around me. In ten minutes I take thirty-six pictures. For each frame, I vary the exposure ever so slightly in the hopes of capturing the high-contrast scene on film—indeed a difficult challenge. Like most professional photographers, I shoot for the great shot and not the snap shots, and I'll be happy to get one great shot per roll. My electronic dive computer indicates that I can safely stay at thirty feet (9 m) for at least another fifteen minutes. I decide to swim away from the reef and hover in blue water.

On my way out of the cave's narrow entrance, I brush the back of my right hand some fire coral, so called because of the burning sensation one gets on contact. The burning is intense, and I know from experience that the sensation will last a day or two. Better be more careful, I tell myself. I am well aware of some of the other

Above: Sunrise on the Reef, Red Sea
Dawn is a time of intense activity on the reef. Nocturnal fishes are searching for places to hide in the reef, while diurnal fishes are just beginning their search for food. During this changing of the guard, all fish are on the lookout for predators, who feed mostly during the half-light periods of sunrise and sunset. Early morning is also a time of great beauty under water.

Opposite: Underwater Cave, Red Sea
Hundreds of sweepers fill many of the caves around Ras Muhammad. When these fish move quickly in unison, a diver can actually hear their fins flutter. Diving the caves in early morning provides dramatic lighting and a visual treat.

potential dangers that lie on the reef: near-invisible stonefish and scorpionfish with dorsal spines that can inflict painful, even deadly, stings; the crown-of-thorns starfish with spines that feel like sharp needles in one's skin; and bristleworms, two-inch-long (5-cm) animals with thousands of hairlike bristles that break off and stick in the skin, causing irritation for several days.

Outside the cave, the calm of the morning is about to be abruptly broken. Fifty or so feet (15 m) away from the reef, perhaps 100- to 150-foot-long (30–45-m) fusiliers are flying in formation along the reef wall, picking out a breakfast of plankton. They see the eight-fish team of two-foot-long (0.6-m) predatory jacks cruising alongside but don't seem to mind their presence—until the attack begins.

Like wolves in a pack, the jacks accelerate together so fast they create a streak in the water. But the fusiliers are quick, too. They explode as they dart out in all directions when the jacks attack, their torpedo-shaped bodies cutting through the water at an equally impressive speed. This time, at least, they reach safe water.

The attacks continue. Then, I'm lucky enough to be looking at the right place at the right time—like when you see a shooting star in a remote part of the sky—when a jack makes a successful strike. The predator bites the smaller fish in half, and the other members of the jack pack swim in to get their share of the prey, tearing it to pieces.

* * *

Lionfish, Red Sea
Lionfish have great camouflage that makes them almost invisible to fish and divers. These predators are usually detected when they move from resting place to resting place, which does not happen often. Lionfish have venomous spines that they use to corral small fishes. Once it has cornered its prey, the lionfish opens its jaws and sucks in the fish.

Raccoon Butterflyfish, Red Sea
The raccoon butterflyfish, shown here, and the bluecheek butterflyfish are two of the most common—and most beautiful—butterflyfish in the Red Sea. During the day, they are difficult to approach. But at night, they "sleep" on the reef, and even the bright light from a camera's strobe doesn't seem to bother them. Perhaps they think it is lightning.

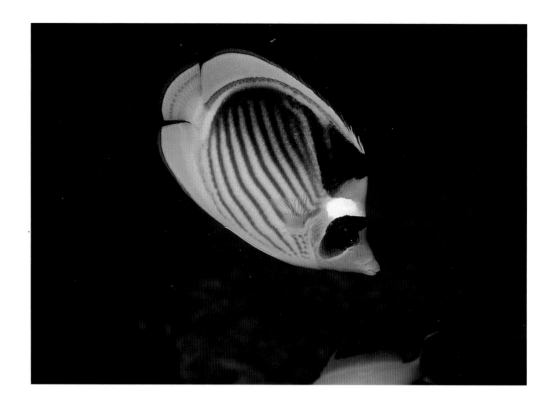

Bluecheek Butterflyfish, Red Sea
Many butterflyfish mate for life, as do some species of birds, including Canada geese. You can tell this picture was taken during the day because the tentacles of the orange cup corals in the background are withdrawn. At night, they extend to trap floating plankton.

During my week in the Red Sea, I completed a series of twenty-seven dives. Our team of nine divers explored, from morning till night, the reefs of Gubal Island, Shaab Abu Nuhas, and Small Passage—all popular sites frequented by dive boats. At Ras Um Sid and the "Temple," near the port of Sharm el Sheikh, the shallow reefs, starting just a few feet below the surface, teem with life, most notably with soft coral formations. And at Alternatives, not too far from Ras Muhammad, massive, silo-shaped castles of hard corals, surrounded by barren sand, attracted dozens of species and hundreds of fish. For me, though, it was the dawn dives at Ras Muhammad that were the most impressive and most inspiring. I can see why my friend marine biologist Dr. Eugenie Clark, noted shark expert, teacher, author, on-site principal investigator on coral reef explorations—and proud grandmother—says that if she could dive in only one place in the world, she would choose Ras Muhammad.

Resting on the bow of the *Colona IV*, I'm inclined to agree with Eugenie. In reviewing my fourteen years of diving, I can't recall seeing so many colorful fish, corals, and other invertebrates—on each and every dive.

It is thanks in part to the efforts of Eugenie, who has explored Ras Muhammad for twenty years, that the rhythm of the reefs here will remain stable. In 1980, she urged President Anwar Sadat of Egypt to declare Ras Muhammad a marine park and limit fishing, outlaw spear fishing, and prohibit shell collecting. After many delays, the park was finally established in 1989. Today, Ras Muhammad National Park is a "must see" for scuba divers the world over—a true Underwater Wonder of the World.

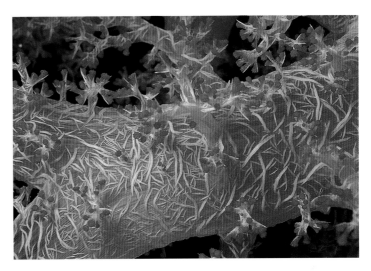

Above: Soft Coral Colony, Red Sea
Close-up photographs reveal the intricate structure of the soft coral colony. In this photograph, dozens of individual animals are visible. During the day, soft corals have few intruders, but at night, tiny spider crabs and barberpole shrimps walk among the protective, stinging tentacles looking for food.

Left: Coral Reef Ecosystem, Red Sea
Coral reefs are one of the most biologically diverse ecosystems on our planet, second only to the tropical rain forest. In the Red Sea, hard and soft corals thrive in year-round warm and sunny weather.

Bannerfish, Red Sea
The bannerfish is easily recognizable on the reef, which is a benefit when looking for a mate. But does this distinctive color pattern make it easy for predators to see this fish, too? Some scientists feel the black and white bars actually make the fish more invisible to predators by breaking up its body pattern, much the way the stripes of a tiger and zebra help these animals avoid detection.

Spotted Moral Eel, Red Sea
Spotted moray eels look threatening, but these animals are actually rather shy and retreat into the safety of the reef when approached by divers. The opening and closing of it mouth is simply the action of the animal forcing water over its gills—in other words, "breathing."

Hawkfish, Red Sea
The freckleface hawkfish lacks a swim bladder, an internal organ that enables free-swimming fishes to hover in water. This bottom dweller is a lay-in-wait predator, with a body pattern that makes it hard for prey to detect. Here it is resting on fire coral, which can inflict a painful sting on a diver's skin.

Chapter 3

Diving at Midday

Truk Lagoon, Micronesia

The hot, bright sun is directly overhead. There are no clouds. No waves. No wind. Perfect conditions for a calm, peaceful dive.

I am in the middle of the Caroline Islands chain in the Federated States of Micronesia in the Pacific Ocean. As I gear up on the dive deck of the *Truk Aggressor*, which has unusually good coffee, I get an eerie feeling when I think that it was on the equally still morning of February 17, 1944, in the mists of World War II, that one hundred American planes, under the code name Operation Hailstorm, descended on a Japanese naval fleet anchored in this strategically located atoll.

The dawn attack took Admiral Koga and his combined fleet of fifty merchant vessels, ten cruisers, twelve submarines, and two aircraft carriers completely by surprise. By the end of the following day, a total of 450 American planes had broken the back of the Japanese Navy. Many Japanese ships were sunk or sinking; four hundred Japanese and twenty-two American planes were downed. The real tragedy was that more than seven hundred people died.

After lying in these shallow, warm, tropical waters for nearly five decades, the now coral-covered ships have become some of the most magnificent artificial reefs in the world, attracting divers from all corners of the globe. My first underwater exploration in Truk will be on the 450-foot-long (135-m) *Fujikawa Maru*. (*Fujikawa* means "mountain rivers" and *Maru* is the designation for merchant ship in Japanese.)

Today's underwater exploration, I know from experience, will not hold too much fast-paced action, because this is the time of day when it is relatively peaceful on the reef. The nocturnal predators—snappers, grunts, bigeyes, eels, and sweepers—have long been back in their lairs, resting after a night of hunting. They, along with larger nighttime feeders such as sharks and stingrays, will not resume their patrols until the sun is near the horizon.

Many diurnal fish, including angelfish, parrotfish, butterflyfish, and clownfish, have been up since dawn and have had their breakfast. Now they may be looking for a snack or for a mate—all the while keeping a vigilant eye out for any fish that might find them a tasty treat. It will be several hours before the sun begins to set and these daylight creatures become more skittish. As dusk falls they have to raise their guard against the threat of fast-

Shipwreck, Truk Lagoon
The mast of the sunken Japanese merchant ship Fujikawa Maru *breaks the surface of the water. Soft corals or algae cover nearly every inch of the mast. Spectacular underwater attractions such as this make Truk a "must see" for scuba divers around the world.*

Poor Man's Moorish Idol,
Truk Lagoon
The shipwrecks of Truk Lagoon
attract many different species
of fish and coral. The
beautiful poor man's moorish
idol is commonly found
swimming alone among the
passageways of the wrecks.

moving night stalkers that begin to search for food in the half light.

I like diving during the relatively peaceful time of midday. This is when it is brightest under water. It is an ideal time for taking in the big picture of the reef and the best time of day for natural-light photography. I check my gauges, hold my face mask, take a breath, and leap off the dive deck into history.

I snorkel over to where the *Fujikawa Maru's* seventy-foot (21-m) main mast still breaks the surface of the water. Beneath me, I can see the ghostly deck, from the stern guns to the port davits. Beyond that, plankton, silt, and sediment cloud the water and the ship becomes a mysterious blur.

As I descend ever so slowly down the mast, I'm awed by the soft corals that seem to bloom in every color of the rainbow—shades of orange, purple, yellow, and red. There are hard corals and sea fans here, too, but it is the soft corals that give this artificial reef, and other Indo-Pacific reefs, their breathtaking color and beauty.

The mast is dotted with dozens of oysters and clams—shellfish that filter plankton and oxygen from the ocean. These marine creatures look harmless enough, especially since they have "cemented" themselves in place for life. However, as they filter large quantities of seawater, concentrations of bacteria, viruses, and biological toxins can build up in the animals' tissues. The danger is especially acute after what is called a *red tide*: an unusually high concentration of toxic microorganisms in the water, sometimes occurring after a rain storm.

According to Dr. Paul S. Auerbach, author of *A Medical Guide to Hazardous Marine Life*, if a contaminated marine animal is eaten, "within hours, there is the onset of numbness and tingling inside and round the mouth. These symptoms progress to the neck, hands, and feet. Other symptoms rapidly develop: weakness, difficulty speaking and swallowing, drooling, thirst, diarrhea, abdominal pain, nausea, vomiting, blurred vision, headache, sweating, chest pain, and rapid heartbeat." According to Dr. Auerbach, 25 percent of victims expire from respiratory failure within the first twelve hours, and he advises people suffering from these symptoms after eating seafood to seek medical attention immediately. I photograph the oysters with their colorful mantles exposed. Then I move on, swearing never to eat shellfish in a foreign country again.

I'm now at 75 feet (22.5 m), floating over the rear deck. I would like to see the ship's huge propeller, but it lies at a depth of 120 feet (36 m). Diving that deep would limit my dive time severely, so I decide to investigate one of the ship's rear holds instead.

Gliding through the huge loading bay to a depth of ninety feet (27 m), my dive light guiding my way through the darkness, I come upon a pile of broken china and bottles. I imagine the ship's crew back in 1944 having breakfast before the air strike, and wonder whether any of them were fathers of young sons, as I am. What was going through their minds as the alarm sounded?

Slowly, I ascend to explore the deck. Poking my head out of the hold, I spot two black-tip reef sharks, and they spot me. I know from experience that sharks, like most fish, are frightened by a diver's bubbles, but I swim toward them anyway to see if I can get a closer look at these sleek predators.

As I expected, they move off the wreck and into the blue of the water. Watching their shadows fade, I think about the shark's bad reputation—and I'm saddened by the fact that each year people kill one hundred million sharks, most for their fins. Poachers catch hundred of sharks at a time on lines that can be up to thirty-five miles (56 km) long. They haul the helpless animals on board and cut off their fins—a practice known as *finning*. They then toss the finless sharks back into the water to die a slow and painful death. The valuable fins are put in the ship's freezer for shipment to the Orient, where they are destined for shark-fin soup, a delicacy in that part of the world

Shipwreck Mast, Truk Lagoon
Descending to the base of the main mast of the Fujikawa Maru, *which is in seventy-five feet (22.5 m) of water, divers encounter several sea anemones and resident clownfish. Sea anemones seldom move, and can live for three hundred years.*

Sharks usually feed at dawn and dusk, so there is no real danger of a shark attacking a diver at midday. However, I always bear in mind that sharks are opportunistic feeders, which means they eat a fish—or on an ever-so-rare occasion, a diver—whenever the hell they want. Other opportunistic predators prowling around the wreck are fierce-looking barracudas and eels, lethargic groupers, jacks in packs, and colorful and dangerous lionfish. But enough of shark chasing. I'm in Truk to photograph shipwrecks, so I move toward the big gun on the ship's bow without taking a picture.

I check around for predators as I take what our skipper, Captain Lenny calls the "scenic route." I enter a passageway on the starboard side of the ship. Dramatic shafts of light penetrate the water and shoot through the now-empty window frames in the roof. In the shadows, I see a group of fifteen or so bright red bigeyes who are seemingly oblivious to my presence. In a few hours, these nocturnal hunters will disband, each seeking out its own prey.

As their name implies, bigeyes are well adapted for nighttime hunting, with big eyes that can see shapes during the night. (It is brighter under water than you may imagine, especially on moonlit nights.) Sight, however, is not the only sense nocturnal fish—or any fish for that matter—use to detect prey. Along the sides of their bodies, all fish have an organ called a lateral line that they use to detect movement. Even in the darkness of night, a fish knows if another fish is approaching, or if it is approaching another fish or a coral head. Fish also use their sense of smell to gather information about their underwater environment. All fish emit amino acids in their excrement and directly through their skin. When other fish smell these substances, they can

Top: Bomber Nosepod, Truk Lagoon
The hulk of the bomber has become home for a school of bannerfish. Swimming inside the nosepod, I became claustrophobic, realizing that the real loss back on that fateful day in 1944 was that of human lives. More than seven hundred people were killed.

Above: "Betty" Bomber, Truk Lagoon
Resting in peace in sixty feet (18 m) of water, this Mitsubishi G4M "Betty" bomber is an eerie testament to Operation Hailstorm. During the allied attack, four hundred Japanese planes and twenty-two American planes were downed.

Left: "Betty" Bomber, Truk Lagoon
The Mitsubishi bomber has been under water for more than fifty years. The nose and cockpit area is severed from the fuselage.

Shipwreck, Truk Lagoon
Diving at midday is the ideal time for natural-light underwater photographs. When the sun is overhead, the underwater world is at its brightest. This mast of the Kensho Maru is a favorite among divers. The diver pictured here is at a depth of about fifty feet (15 m); at this depth, he can explore the wreck for about an hour.

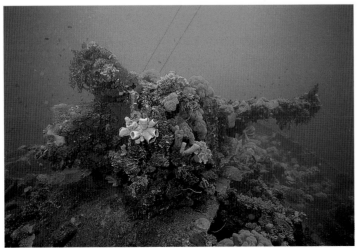

Above: Japanese Tank, Truk Lagoon
Weapons of war now lay silent on the shipwrecks of Truk Lagoon. On the Nippon Maru, *this tank lies at 115 feet (34.5 m).*

Left: Bow Gun on Shipwreck, Truk Lagoon
Artificial coral reefs have grown over most of the war's remains, turning swords into plowshares. The bow gun of the Fujikawa Maru *is a thriving mini-reef in only forty feet (12 m) of water.*

Truck Remains, Truk Lagoon
Lying under water for more than fifty years, this coral-covered Japanese military truck is barely recognizable—it's become a home for several species of hard and soft corals, sponges, oysters, algae, and fish.

Remnants of War, Truk Lagoon
The holds of the ghost ships of Truk Lagoon are filled with remnants of war—unused bullets and a ship's china. Like all the other bullets, bombs, and shells that lie in the wrecks of Truk Lagoon, the bullets are still considered "live ammo" and should not be handled.

Remnants of War, Truk Lagoon
Truk Lagoon is a protected park, and artifacts—such as this ship's store of china—may not be removed. Corals can't grow on artifacts such as these deep within the ships' rooms and holds for two reasons: There's little light, and a silt covering prevents corals from gaining a foothold.

determine the fish's species, size, and perhaps even its level of stress.

My ability to explore the reef is limited to what I can see and touch. Turning over a tattered gas mask, I startle a small octopus. In the blink of an eye, the octopus propels itself out one of the window openings by pumping water through its siphon. At first, the animal looks dark brown, but when it lands on the green deck, it immediately changes color and texture to match its surroundings, making it almost invisible to me—and to potential predators.

I leave the passageway and float over the top of the pilot house, where I am greeted by the bright sunlight that lights this section of ship even at a depth of thirty-five feet (10.5 m). Carpeting the port and starboard davits are colorful soft coral colonies. Corals use their tentacles to trap plankton in the water. Unlike most hard corals, which extend their tentacles at night to feed, most soft corals ex-

tend their tentacles throughout the day and night, making them round-the-clock colorful subjects for underwater photographers.

I photograph the davits in natural light and with a flash. At this depth, the water has filtered out most of the colors we normally see, so the structures, as well as the entire wreck, have a blue tint when photographed in natural light. This is how reefs at this depth look to fish. When I use a flash, which creates daylight lighting conditions, the colors come alive.

When I photograph reefs, I use a wide-angle lens that lets me get close to the subject. The closer you get, the less water there is between you and your subject. This is important for sharp underwater pictures because the density of water means the farther you are from your subject, the softer your pictures will be. Water is full of plankton and other floating particles that cloud the scene. In

Above: Interior of "Betty" Bomber, Truk Lagoon
Algae and fish now make their home in the encrusted interior of the Mitsubishi *bomber.*

Left: Ship's Pilot House, Truk Lagoon
"Full speed ahead." "Rudder, hard left." Echoes of long-ago commands ring in my head as I explore the pilot house of the Kensho Maru. *The once-active ship's telegraph is now frozen for all time.*

addition, water not only filters out color vertically—meaning the deeper you go, the less color you see—it also filters out color horizontally. Therefore, the closer you are to your subject, the more color you will be able to record on film.

Twenty minutes have passed, and I have only about fifteen minutes of dive time remaining. The bow gun is already in sight so I decide to continue my swim forward. As I float over forward hold number two, I spot the faint, twisted remains of a Japanese fighter plane. The hold is dark, but my dive light casts a bright, narrow beam on the plane. Silt and sediment completely cover the fighter; there is no coral growth anywhere. The plane's last resting place is too dark for corals, which need plenty of light to grow. Corals also require a constant supply of plankton to feed on. These microscopic planklets usually drift by the corals on currents and surges. But down here the water is dead still. The constant drizzle of silt and sediment in the eerie silence forms a soft coating on the plane that prevents corals from gaining the strong foothold they would need to begin a colony even if they could survive down here.

I photograph the plane and notice that I have only ten exposures left. Then I check my gauges and see that I have been under water for about a half hour. I need to begin my ascent in about five minutes or I will have to make a decompression stop to release the nitrogen dissolved in my bloodstream before surfacing. I want to avoid getting nitrogen narcosis, which makes one feel drunk and therefore an unsafe diver. I move on quickly to photograph the bow gun, which was my main reason for diving this wreck in the first place.

The gun with its colorful drapery of soft corals and sponges is truly magnificent. At a length of about fifteen feet (4.5 m), it is an impressive reminder that in times of war, even merchant ships are capable of inflicting damage when threatened. Darting around over the barrel are dozens of two-inch-long (5-cm) damselfish, feeding on plankton as it drifts by. When the light begins to fade in a few hours, these fish, like most relatively small reef fish, will seek shelter in the nooks and crannies of the surrounding artificial reef. For now, they add a touch of beauty and motion to the scene I see in my viewfinder.

I make my last exposure, and then I notice a bright red lionfish leaving its resting place at the base of the gun. A photograph of this fish would have been an impressive addition to my pictures of the gun, but I have to resign myself to one of the realities of underwater photography: The really great underwater picture opportunities happen when you are out of film—or when you have the wrong lens on your camera.

* * *

The *Fujikawa Maru* offers many of the sights a diver would see on the fifty or so other accessible wrecks in Truk. But if you are thinking, "If you've seen one wreck, you've seen them all," you'll be pleasantly surprised if you ever go to Truk. The *Nippon Maru* offers among its subjects three artillery cannons, a tank, and a truck body; the *Kensho Maru* is an upright wreck with perhaps the most impressive pilot house, complete with coral-covered telegraph; the *Shinkoku Maru* has the most prolific marine life of all the wrecks I've dived; and the deck of the *Sankisan Maru*, a ship that was cut literally in half by a bomb, is littered with bullets, machine guns, and medicine and sake bottles.

* * *

My last dive in Truk is on a Mitsubishi G4M "Betty" bomber, a relatively intact twin-engine plane lying on a patch of white sand in about sixty feet (18 m) of water. Again, I am diving at midday to maximize my opportunities for natural-light photography.

My exploration of the wreckage begins at the plane's rear doorway. As I swim through the opening, I notice that virtually all the plane's contents have been removed. Hovering in mid-plane is a school of butterflyfish that dart out of sight when they see this strange creature breathing bubbles and creating bursts of lightning with the weird apparatus in his hands.

As I enter the cockpit, a green moray eel pokes its head out from under the pilot's seat. It looks very ferocious, opening and

Opposite: Fighter Plane Cockpit, Truk Lagoon
In the dark number two hold of the Fujikawa Maru, *remains of a Japanese fighter plane remind me of man's inhumanity to man. The hold in which this plane lies is almost completely dark, and divers need artificial light to see and photograph it.*

closing its mouth and showing its razor-sharp teeth. Dr. Ernie Ernst has told me that these fish are actually quite shy and tend to back away from divers. True to form, the eel retreats into its hiding place as I approach.

Ernie also told me the reason all moray eels open and close their mouths in this way is that, unlike other fish, their gills are located in their throats and not on the outside of their bodies. This means they must constantly pump water through their mouths to get a fresh supply of oxygen to their gills. This action makes them look more threatening than they actually are.

Ernie gave me another interesting fact about the green moray: It is not green at all—it is blue. The eel is covered with a yellow slimy mucus that makes it look green. This mucous coating is very important to eels and indeed to all fish. It not only acts as a lubricant that helps the fish move swiftly through the water, but it also helps protect the animal from infections and parasites. This is why you should not touch a fish when you are diving, for if the mucous coating is rubbed off, the fish becomes more susceptible to disease. The slimy mucous coating also seals the fish's semipermeable body, which prevents the fish's internal salt concentrations from rising (through osmosis) to match the concentration of the surrounding seawater. If fish were not watertight, they would leak water and dehydrate.

The eel makes one more wide-open yawn. On the inside of the animal's mouth I notice two tiny red-banded coral shrimps scurrying around. I know why they are there, because I've dived numerous times with Dr. Mary Wicksten of Texas A&M University, principal investigator on several CEDAM International expeditions. Mary is an expert on cleaner shrimps—shrimps that clean parasites and dead scales off a willing fish's body. She notes that these shrimps are essential for keeping fish healthy—a reminder that every species, even the smallest, is essential to the reef's survival.

I make my exit through the cockpit and photograph the wreck site in its entirety. I also photograph some of the items that were thrown from the plane when it hit the water—one engine, a cannon, a toilet seat, machine guns, and the co-pilot's seat.

Now I'm almost out of air and need to surface. As usual, time

Coral Garden on Shipwreck, Truk Lagoon
Lush soft-coral gardens entirely cover the bow deck of the Nippon Maru. *The ship lies almost upright on the sandy bottom, and you can see the bow rails if you look hard enough.*

has moved all too fast under water for this air-breathing creature. I must leave this world, where I am weightless and can freely move in three dimensions rather than the two I am restricted to on land. Back on the dive deck I hear the buzz of a Continental island hopper flying overhead. I look up and spot the faint silhouette of the small plane—or is it the ghost of a Japanese Zero making a run for it?

Above: Lifeboat Davits on Shipwreck, Truk Lagoon
These davits, used to lower lifeboats into the water, are today covered with beautiful soft corals. I took this picture on an unusually clear day with an ultra-wide-angle lens, which allowed me get to within a few feet of the foreground davits while maintaining a focused background.

Left: Noon on the Reef, Truk Lagoon
Anemones and anemonefish are common sights on the shipwrecks of Truk. This anemone is on the mast of the ship Kensho Maru *at a depth of forty-five feet (13.5 m).*

Chapter 4

Twilight Descends

Cocos Island, Costa Rica

We are anchored in Chatham Bay on the lee side of Cocos Island in the Pacific Ocean far off Costa Rica. It has been raining hard since dawn and a moderate wind from the north adds a chill to the late-afternoon air. The water around our mother ship, the 120-foot (36-m) *Okeanos Aggressor*, is calm, but as I look over to our dive site, on Manuelita Island's windward side, I see whitecaps. It will be a rough ten-minute ride in our ten-man Zodiac, which is good news for neither my stomach nor my camera equipment, both of which are sensitive.

As our team gears up, Mario Arroyo, the *Okeanos*'s dive master, tells us we must all enter the water at the same time, paratrooper style, to avoid being separated by the strong surface current. "The currents are strong in Cocos," he cautions. "Within a minute or two, you can lose your buddy — especially when visibility is low as it is today. If you run into a problem under water, you're out of luck if you're alone." His face brightens with a warm smile and a laugh. "That was the serious news. The good news is that you're in for an underwater experience that can't be beat. In Cocos, we guarantee white-tip sharks, hammerhead sharks, and huge schools of bigeye jacks." He continues, "But we don't guarantee they won't bite you."

During his briefing, Mario also tells us that we will probably see Galápagos and silky sharks, hawksbill turtles, as well as marbled and manta rays. "Now let's go and get some great photographs," says the confident leader of our dive team. "*Vámanos!*"

In the pouring rain, we ride over bumpy waves to our dive site. The conditions do not dampen our spirits one bit. Our team of CEDAM International expeditioners came to Cocos prepared for what is called "adventure diving," and we are about to experience it. Mario, Gonzalo Gonzalez (CEDAM's representative in Costa Rica), and I are the first in the water. We descend quickly together, while the rest of the team follows shortly behind. At sixty feet (18 m), with visibility limited to forty feet (12 m), we are alone; the current has taken us away from the others. We signal to each other that we are OK, and Mario leads us on our dive.

As the current carries us along, a huge, dark cloud looms ahead, a sight I have never seen before. As we move closer, I make out a school of fish. At first I wonder whether they could they be hammerheads; then the outlines of the bigeye jacks come into view.

In a few breaths, I am swimming inside the school, which is moving effortlessly against the strong current. All I can see are two-

Manta Ray and Divers, Cocos Island
Manta rays are among the most graceful animals in the sea, flapping their "wings" as they fly over the reef.
In Cocos, mantas and other fish are protected, but in some parts of the world, mantas are caught
accidentally in drift nets and on long lines.

foot-long (0.6-m) jacks—up, down, everywhere. Three hundred fish, maybe more, surround me. I photograph the school, which blocks out what little sunlight there is, in both natural light and with my flash. In natural light I record how the fish look to themselves, to predators, and to prey; with the flash I shoot for the details on their highly reflective silver bodies. Thrilled to be diving with jacks, which could easily rip off an ear or a finger if they were to decide it was food, I shoot twenty-four pictures to capture the wonder of such an underwater encounter.

The jacks move on, and I'm left with a feeling of frustration that I will probably never see hammerheads schooling in these waters. Some experts estimate that in the last twenty years the shark population around Cocos has decreased by as much as 70 percent. Several years ago the decrease in shark sightings was blamed on warmer waters around the island driving sharks deeper and farther from shore to cooler water. It is now acknowledged that the real reason for the decline is illegal fishing, mostly by foreign fishing vessels in search of shark fins. Cocos was established as a national park in 1978, and fishing and shell collecting are prohibited within a five-mile (8-km) radius of the island. But with only five rangers and two boats smaller than our Zodiac, it is impossible to patrol these waters effectively.

I hear a *tap, tap, tap,* and look around to see who is banging on his scuba tank. Mario is pointing to a section of the near-vertical wall that we are cruising along. At least ten white-tip sharks are attacking something that is trying to escape into the reef. I swim into the shark feeding-frenzy to get a photograph, but the sharks have already devoured their prey and are beginning to disperse. One four-foot-long (1.2-m) white-tip grazes my head with his pectoral fin as he exits the scene of the massacre. Although sharks seldom attack divers, I'm thankful that I am bigger than these are. I also feel fortunate to have witnessed a natural feeding frenzy—as opposed to those seen on television where sharks are driven crazy by blood and guts poured in the water—because a shark can survive for months between meals, living off fat stored in its liver.

We move on. We are now at the end of the near-vertical wall

Manuelita Island
Divers reach Manuelita Island off Cocos Island via an inflatable boat, launched from a mother ship anchored in Chatham Bay. On a single tank of air, a diver staying at a depth of about forty feet (12 m) can completely swim around the island in less than an hour. The facing lee side hosts less marine life than the rougher windward side on the opposite side of the island.

on the rough side of Manuelita and, as planned, we swim around the point to the almost dead-calm lee side. We have about fifteen minutes of air left, so we explore the shallows to see what reef creatures are out in the late-afternoon hours.

Although many divers come to Cocos for the "biggies," the close-up world offers many wonders, too. In the thirty-foot (9-m) shallows, we pass several schools of convict tangs and gold-rimmed surgeonfish, with up to fifty fish in each school. The fish swim slowly just a few inches over the reef and then, as if on cue, descend in unison onto the algae-covered rocks, where they begin feeding. In a few hours, these schools will disband and the individual fish will seek out solitary sleeping places in the reef. I photograph them, even though I know a two-dimensional image cannot really capture the amazing sight of so many fish in one place at one time.

Waterfall, Cocos Island
The average annual rainfall in Cocos is 250 to 300 inches (625–750 cm), creating a beautiful and lush tropical island dotted with dozens of waterfalls.

flounders lie camouflaged on the sandy bottom. These strange fish are born with eyes on both sides of their heads; as they mature, one eye migrates to the other side, making them look like creatures from another planet. Three-inch-long (7.5-cm) red-light blennies lie motionless in the shallows while their eyes pivot around on the lookout for food and danger. Fine-spotted moray eels, still tucked safely away in their rock dwellings, will soon be leaving for a night of feeding on crabs, octopuses, and lobsters.

One daytime feeder has already bedded down for the night. It is an azure parrotfish tucked under a rocky ledge that affords some protection from larger predators. It seems to be staring at me with its large eyes, but I get to within inches of the animal and it seems oblivious to my presence. I get a good look at the fish's beaklike jaw, which it uses to chomp off pieces of algae from rock-hard surfaces. It is the

Cocos does indeed have lots of fish. Fellow expeditioner John Rothman explains it like this. "Since Cocos is an oceanic island, it has relatively few fish species, but the numbers of fish are great. And because of its isolation, several endemic species have evolved. Most of the species, however, are shared with the shores of the Central American mainland and the Galápagos Islands, but many are of Indo-Pacific origin. Scientists speculate that the reef fish that successfully colonize oceanic islands such as Cocos are species that have long larval stages or that are able to retard development of adult characteristics. By remaining as pre-adults, the fish can travel with the oceanic currents as plankton feeders and avoid the need for a reef environment until one becomes available."

There are bottom dwellers and feeders here, too. Leopard

unique eating adaptations of reef inhabitants such as this one, and their correspondingly selective diets, that enable the ecosystem to survive despite the combination of hundreds of different species of fish and invertebrates with a limited food supply.

The light is fading now and Mario signals that it is time to go up. Gonzalo and I give the OK, and we make our way toward the silhouette of the dive boat. When we break the surface, we are greeted by rain. It feels good, but we sure do wish the sun was shining. Even though we are wearing full wet suits and the water is 82°F (28°C), we are cold. (People lose body heat faster in water than in air, and even in relatively warm water most divers get cold.) We all are eager to get back to the *Okeanos*, take a hot shower, have a cup of coffee, and share our dive experiences with the other

Jack School, Cocos Island
Schools of jack, sometimes comprising hundreds of fish, are a common late-afternoon sight off the Cocos. Fish school when hunting and for protection against larger predators such as sharks.

expeditioners.

Like all CEDAM International projects, the Cocos project is conservation oriented. Our objectives include producing a slide show and videotape for school children in Costa Rica; publishing a special issue of the CEDAM International newsletter, *Reef Explorer*, and a small guide book on the fish and invertebrates of Cocos; and donating up to one thousand slides to the Costa Rica national parks, which were established by former president Lic Rodrigo Carazo, whom we met before we set out for Cocos. Our team includes writers, videographers, and photographers, all ready, willing, and able to help achieve the project's goals.

Cocos is the largest uninhabited island in the world.

Manuelita was a favorite dive site for most of us. (If you've seen the movie *Jurassic Park*, you have seen Manuelita: It is the island in the movie's opening sequence.) We also explored the other popular dive sites, including Submerged Rock, Pajara (Bird) Island, and Dirty Rock, the latter so called because of all the bird guano that covers the rocky outcroppings.

The most distinguishing feature of this underwater environment, besides the prolific fish life, is the absence of the lush coral reefs we are used to seeing in the Pacific, Red Sea, and Caribbean. As in the Galápagos Islands, which are only about six hundred miles (960 km) southwest of Cocos, there are few hard corals and virtually no soft corals in Cocos, although the lee side of Pajara

Above: Azure Parrotfish, Cocos Island
Parrotfish have specially adapted jaws that let them chew on hard coral. While swimming along a reef, divers can hear this chomping; those with a trained eye will also notice the fish's teeth marks on the hard coral.

Left: Underwater Rock Ledge, Cocos Island
Although Cocos supports a healthy fish population, it doesn't support lush coral growth. Periodically, when a change in the weather pattern called El Niño (The Child) occurs, the water becomes too warm and the corals die. The last El Niño occurred in 1982–1983.

Above: Blue-Striped Snapper School, Cocos Island
"A wall of fish" is the only way I can describe this school of blue-striped snappers. I stopped counting the fish—which surrounded me for about ten minutes—when I got to one hundred.

Right: Lobster, Cocos Island
The Cocos spiny lobster lacks the fierce-looking claws of its "cousin," the North American Maine lobster. These bottom-dwellers spend the day hiding in the nooks and crannies of the reef; at night, they scavenge the sandy bottom for clams, mussels, snails, and starfish. Lobsters lay between three thousand and ten thousand eggs at a time, but the survival rate is low due to the many fish that eat the eggs.

Above: Hiding Marbled Ray, Cocos Island
Marbled rays hide from predatory sharks by burrowing themselves in the sand. These fish "fly" though the water only a few feet above the reef by slowly flapping their wings; the wings can have a span of up to six feet (1.8 m). Off Cocos, divers can also encounter eagle rays and manta rays.

Left: White-Tip Shark, Cocos Island
Startled by my bubbles, which make a relatively loud sound under water, this small white-tip shark darts out of a cave, where I saw it attacking a fish. With standard scuba gear, getting close to sharks is difficult due to the warning given by your air bubbles.

Island does have a section of healthy hard coral. Cool water in Galápagos (65–70°F/18–21°C) retards coral growth in that archipelago, but the water around Cocos (75–82°F/24–28°C) is warm enough to support coral reefs. Coral around Cocos is sparse because periodically the water becomes too warm. Every few years, a warm-weather pattern known as El Niño (The Child) strikes the waters around both Cocos and Galápagos; in 1982–1983, El Niño was particularly pronounced and it killed most of the corals in both areas.

Under water, divers encounter sheer vertical cliffs, walls, and drop-offs, as well as clusters of huge boulders. Bob Snodgrass, Collections Curator at the Steven Birch Aquarium, Scripps Institute of Oceanography, University of California, San Diego, who is the principal investigator on this trip, explains the origins of Cocos Island. "Tracing the geological history of an extinct volcanic island such as Isla del Coco is a difficult task. It lies just northwest of the Cocos Ridge, running across the Cocos Plate, which is slowly moving northeast from the Galápagos 'hot spot' (a plume of magma rising from the earth's interior that persists for millions of years at the same location) to the submarine trench where it sinks under Central America. The ridge is believed to represent a trace of this hotspot, deduced by sampling along its length and plate-motion studies. Cocos Island, several million years younger than the nearby portion of the ridge, is chemically similar to it. This indicates that although not produced directly by the hotspot, it could have been derived from leftover plume materials trapped under the Cocos Ridge. These have remelted and escaped through faults caused by stress as the ridge clogs the subduction zone at the isthmus. Many

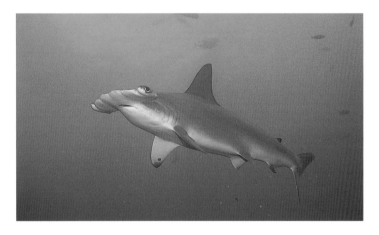

Above: Hammerhead Shark, Cocos Island
This lone hammerhead shark is on its way to a cleaning station, where a school of barberfish will pick parasites from the animal's body—without fear of being eaten. In Cocos, huge schools of hammerhead sharks used to be common. Now, this sight is rare because of uncontrolled shark fishing; experts estimate the shark population in Cocos has decreased by 70 percent in the past twenty years.

Right: Pacific Seahorse, Cocos Island
Cocos has some of the largest seahorses in the world. This Pacific seahorse is about four inches (10 cm) tall, but can grow to a height of twelve inches (30 cm). I found it just where our dive guide said it had been for months, curled around a broken branch on the lee side of Manuelita Island in about fifteen feet (4.5 m) of water.

similar young volcanoes lie along the ridge but have never reached the surface to form islands. The geology of the Cocos Ridge is still a matter of debate. Scientists do not yet know if the faults in the ridge penetrate the earth's crust clear through the mantle, or merely weaken it, allowing the magma to rise through it."

* * *

This afternoon and evening, the final day of our eight-day live-aboard adventure, we are scheduled to dive at Submerged Rock. Excitement is high, as the site is a favorite of the crew's. It will be our last adventure in Cocos before the dreaded thirty-six-hour boat ride back to Puntarenas on the west coast of Costa Rica, a ride that on the way out had many of us glued to our bunks for hours at a time.

Once again we are in the Zodiac, and once again it is raining. CEDAM had booked this trip for the end of October because that is supposed to be the end of the rainy season in Cocos. Dr. Suzanne Pitts, one of our divers, explains with a smile: "Cocos gets about 250 to 300 inches [625–750 cm] of rainfall each year, with a nine-month rainy season followed by a three-month wet season. So, I guess you could say the rainy season runs from January 1 to December 31." We all laugh ruefully as the waves splash into our inflatable Zodiac making us, if possible, even wetter.

In the middle of what seems like nowhere, our dive master for the day, Alberto Munzo, signals to Francisco Marin, the captain of the *Okeanos* and driver of the Zodiac, to cut the engine. "We're here," he says. "Everyone in the water." We look around for a reference point but see none. Alberto explains that we are over Submerged Rock, which is located by using two reference points on land, at least a mile (1.6 km) away.

Gonzalo and I are diving buddies again today, and we descend rapidly to about thirty feet (9 m) to see the top of an almost cylindrical rock with a diameter of about one hundred feet (30 m). As we slowly descend around the rock, we encounter a squadron of sixteen marbled rays flying in formation. Gonzalo and I fly with

the squad for a few minutes and photograph these graceful animals in their underwater ballet. As we move on, I remember one of the golden rules of getting good underwater pictures: Keep looking around—up, down, sideways. The photo opportunities are usually there; it is the ever-alert photographer who gets the shot.

Following this rule, I scan the area. Luck is with me. In the open water I see an eight-foot-long (2.4-m) scalloped hammerhead shark approaching. Then I see the largest white-tip I have encountered on this trip—it must be six to seven feet (1.8–2.1 m). Both animals are framed against a light blue background. I wait patiently and hope they will come to me because I know that chasing after them is impossible. Like many sharks, however, these two are scared off by the bubbles from our scuba tanks and, although I get good photographs, they are not the full-frame images I had hoped for.

About halfway around the rock, at a depth of seventy feet (21 m), Gonzalo turns and points to a cave that runs through the middle of the mammoth structure. He leads the way through a strong surge, and I follow. I spot a white-tip resting or sleeping on the sandy bottom of the cave. I remember reading years ago that sharks have to keep moving (to pump water over their gills) to survive. As with a good number of other early "ocean facts," this statement is obviously incorrect. When I take a picture, my flash startles the animal and in a split second it vanishes. If it was sleeping, it sure as hell woke up fast, I say to myself.

In the cave, I also spot a pink-lipped scorpionfish with dorsal spines that can inflict a painful or even deadly sting. The surge in the cave is pushing me toward this dangerous animal, and I struggle to avoid contact. The surge makes me feel as though I were in a washing machine, but I make it out of the cave with only a few bruises on my legs and arms.

Heading toward the surface, I'm rewarded for clean living: I see a manta ray with a wing span of at least ten feet (3 m) fly overhead. It is a beautiful sight and the perfect end to a perfect dive trip—even if it did rain just about all day every day.

Barracuda School, Cocos Island
Barracuda usually swim in large, polarized schools, meaning that they swim in the same direction and at the same speed. Approaching these predators—who can swim at lighting-fast speeds and who have razor-sharp teeth—is difficult.

Left: Convictfish School, Cocos Island
Convictfish, also called convict tangs, always travel in schools just a few inches above the reef. At some signal, the entire school descends, like a squadron of dive bombers, on the reef, nibbling on patches of algae.

Opposite: Hieroglyphic Hawkfish, Cocos Island
I'm often amazed at the camouflage patterns on a fish's body. This hieroglyphic hawkfish, for example, has a wild body pattern that helps it avoid detection from predators. It's only with the aid of artificial light, which adds contrast and detail to underwater scenes, that this bottom-dwelling fish becomes more visible.

Above: Goldrimmed Surgeonfish, Cocos Island
Goldrimmed surgeonfish get their name from the golden edging of their ventral and dorsal fins and the scalpel-sharp projections in front of their tails, which act as a deterrent to larger fish. From the side, these fish appear to have large bodies, which may offer some protection from predators. Head-on, however, this fish's width — about one inch (2.5 cm) — is revealed.

Left: Fine-Spotted Moray Eel, Cocos Island
During daylight hours the fine-spotted moray eel backs its long body into a hole in the reef, usually leaving only its head exposed. In the late afternoon, this sleek fish emerges from its lair; at night, it prowls the reef looking for octopuses, shellfish, and other reef dwellers. By dawn, it's tucked back safely in its same hiding place. Many nocturnal fish live in the same place for a long time, sharing it with a diurnal fish.

Chapter 5

The Midnight Sea
Bonaire, The Netherlands Antilles

A cloak of darkness surrounds us, so all depth and distance references—surface, sandy bottom, and reef—are eliminated. In this peaceful, black abyss, we feel as though we are floating in deep space. Off somewhere in the distance we see a faint glow that looks like twinkling stars on a clear night. We have seen this beautiful light show before on night dives. It is created by bioluminescent algae disturbed by an underwater current or the wake of a fish.

We are experiencing the beauty and drama of being in the underwater world well after dark in a way often missed by scuba divers—without activating our underwater flashlights. It is a unique, thrilling, alone feeling that is not for everyone. Could there be a tiger shark or a great barracuda swimming alongside us, or some other predator with razor-sharp teeth on the lookout for a midnight snack?

On this underwater adventure I am aware that, day or night, there is always the potential for danger—from predatory fish, malfunctioning equipment, the bends, nitrogen narcosis, or getting lost or trapped on a reef or wreck. I think I agree with Marco Polo, one of the most famous explorers of all time, who once said: "There is no real adventure without danger."

As we follow our compass reading toward our destination, lights from above softly illuminate several ominous-looking, parallel columns that rise from the sea floor to the surface. As we near the structures, we switch on our dive lights and are ready to explore what many divers, including ourselves, consider one of the best night dives in the Caribbean: the Bonaire Town Pier.

My wife and I have chosen this site in the Netherlands Antilles to illustrate the beauty of a night dive for good reason: The pier, surrounded by calm water, acts like a powerful magnet for marine life. The pilings are covered with several species of hard coral, including beautiful orange cup corals; red, orange, and green tube sponges; flowerlike featherduster worms; and loggerhead sponges. Living in and around this magnificent artificial reef are dozens of species of reef fish and invertebrates, most notably crabs. With this diversity of marine life and rainbow of colors, the Bonaire Town Pier is an underwater photographer's paradise—with the coral-

Schooling Fish, Bonaire
Many divers consider the Bonaire Town Pier to be the best night dive in the Caribbean. During daylight hours large schools of fish dart between the numerous columns of this thriving artificial reef. Divers visiting Bonaire should make a day dive under the pier before exploring it at night, when they could get confused about where they are in relationship to their boat or the shore.

covered pillars just a five-minute swim from shore.

What's more, Bonaire and the two other islands in the ABC island chain, Aruba and Curaçao, are well out of the hurricane belt, so the weather is good all year around. In fact, Bonaire advertises good diving 365 days a year—a claim that is not possible to make in most Caribbean dive destinations.

The pier and the waters surrounding Bonaire are a conservationist's dream come true. In 1979, the Netherlands Antilles National Parks Foundation received a grant from the World Wildlife Fund to set up the Bonaire Marine Park to preserve the pristine coral reef ecosystem. Today, the reefs—artificial and natural—are a testament to the benefit of conservation programs, which in this case prohibit commercial and spear fishing (fishing for personal consumption is allowed); collecting of fish, shells, and corals; and anchoring (all boats must use permanent moorings). Thanks to the efforts of the marine park management, which enjoys the support of local dive operators, the rhythm of the reef here should go unchanged for years to come.

Checking my depth gauge, I see that we are at forty feet (12 m). As I scan the sandy bottom with my light, I catch sight of a spotted moray eel, a predator that hides in the reef by day and goes on patrol shortly after the sun sets. Unlike most other nocturnal fish, which have eyes well adapted for seeing in the dark, the eel has poor vision. It compensates for this with a keen sense of smell. Its especially long nasal grooves can detect injured or sleeping prey for up to several yards.

Above: French Grunts and Soldierfish, Bonaire
These French grunts, also known as yellowfish, and black-bar soldierfish have found a safe daytime hiding place in these two tires under the Bonaire Town Pier. After nightfall, they'll prowl the area around the pier in search of food.

Right: Town Pier, Bonaire
During daylight the Bonaire Town Pier is a hub of activity. Tugs and fishing boats come and go, and locals on the dock drop lines in the hope of catching dinner. To dive the Pier you need to make arrangements with the dock master, who knows the arrival and departure schedule of the tugs. Still, divers—as always—should be aware of what's happening all around them when they are diving. Accidents can happen.

Night Dive Under a Full Moon, Bonaire
Night diving under a full moon is an enthralling experience. Surprisingly to non-divers, it's bright enough to see under water without a light on nights like this. A diver needs a light, however, for two reasons: to bring out the true colors of the reef and its creatures, and for safety.

The hunt has begun. Seemingly oblivious to our presence and our lights, the eel flies gracefully through the water and around the columns. Resting on a nearby sponge is what looks like an easy meal—a sleeping, foot-long (0.3-m) stoplight parrotfish. The eel passes it by. The reason for this seeming oversight is that the parrotfish has a unique cloaking device. Each night, the parrotfish secretes a transparent, mucous cocoon that hides its smell from predators. According to scientists, the parrotfish needs this protective device because it is one of the few fish that falls into a deep sleep at night the way we do. Other fish, they say, are in a state of half-sleep, which is beneficial when predators are lurking around.

The eel disappears into the darkness, and we turn our investigation toward the largest pilings at the end of the pier. Suddenly, I feel a tug at my back. I turn around and realize that I am entangled in monofilament fishing line, probably cut free by one of the local anglers who frequent the pier. I try to free the line, but I get more and more entangled. Susan is ahead of me and unaware of my predicament. Strange as it may sound, divers have drowned after getting snagged in line under water. If you cannot free yourself, you eventually run out of air. I am well aware of this danger and always dive with a dive knife to cut myself loose. I disentangle myself from the cut line and join Susan, who is looking intently at something on the piling. It is a subject that, because of its excellent ability to blend in with its surroundings, has consistently eluded me and my cameras for fourteen years of night diving: a longsnout seahorse.

I photograph the three-inch-tall (7.5-cm), orange fish and advance my film to the next frame. But while composing the next picture, I see that the fish has now turned yellow. Then, as I focus, it becomes dark brown. This color change is one of the amazing

Orange Cup Coral, Bonaire
After the sun sets, the pilings of the Bonaire Town Pier come alive with brilliant colors. Orange cup corals, whose polyps open at night, live on many of the pilings, and do not appear in large colonies on the open reef. This species of coral thrives in shady areas, whereas most corals thrive where there is plenty of sunlight. As you can see, marine life covers virtually every inch of this piling.

91

Life on Piling, Bonaire
Artificial reefs, like natural coral reefs, are permanent homes for countless animals—and should be left untouched. Here, a trumpetfish hides in the branches of a rope sponge, while a school of silversides darts behind the piling. The line you see around the rope sponge is holding the sponge in place, in the hope that it will reattach itself to the piling (sponges here were removed in an effort to "clean up" the pier). A Bonaire naturalist named Dee Scarr has spearheaded the reattaching project, an important effort to save this thriving artificial reef.

camouflage techniques the animal uses to avoid detection by predators; the other is a covering of algae and microorganisms that grows on its hard body, making it almost invisible on the reef—to predators and scuba divers alike. The seahorse is amazing for yet another reason: Eggs deposited by the female are fertilized in the male's pouch, where they stay until they hatch. So, it is the male seahorse that becomes "pregnant."

Swimming beneath the pier and back toward shore, I make a photographic catalog of the marine life. I am grateful to have Susan, my diving buddy and photo assistant, with me. She not only helps me find reef creatures, but also carries two extra cameras, giving me a total of 108 frames on three rolls of film to shoot.

The water is getting shallow now, and I could stand if I wanted to. Even at this depth, however, there is plenty of marine life. Orange cup corals, which are not common in the Caribbean, virtually cover some of the pilings, making us feel as if we were walking in a beautiful flower garden. Crabs are everywhere, including several species of decorator crabs, which clip off pieces of sponge and other organisms and attach them to their shells as camouflage.

Red-tipped fireworms, which have hairlike spines that can inflict a painful sting that lasts for days, and scorpionfish, with dorsal spines that can also cause divers pain, are here, too. There are even sea slugs, or nudibranchs, distant relatives of the ugly slugs that we find in our backyard. These creatures, however, are among the most beautiful animals in the sea. And, like many underwater invertebrates, they mostly come out of the reef at night, when a cloak of

Seahorse, Bonaire
Seahorses are masters of camouflage, changing color to match their surroundings. Seahorses are also hard to detect because they move so seldom, allowing camouflaging algae to grow on their hard bodies. To find a seahorse, look at the base of soft coral trees. Unless you have a keen eye, however, you may be looking at a seahorse and never know it.

darkness conceals them.

The photo opportunities on the pier are endless, but now I am out of film and we are low on air. It's time to get back to the hotel to prepare for our second dive on the pier tonight. It might seem like a tight schedule, but an important part of getting good pictures is spending as much time as possible under water, as that increases one's chances of being in the right place at the right time. I am grateful to have such an understanding wife and diving partner to keep up with me on these trips, and I give her much of the credit for my underwater pictures.

* * *

We were in Bonaire for one week, making a total of five night dives on the Bonaire Town Pier and three on Klein Bonaire, a small island about a ten-minute boat ride from the dock in front of our hotel.

The open-water reef explorations on Klein are more adventurous than dives on the town pier. The reef here runs as deep as 130 feet (39 m), which is far too deep for these parents of a three-year-old to dive. In the darkness of night, without a surface reference point, and without constantly checking a depth gauge, it is possible to dive too deep without realizing it. Another consideration for open-water diving—day and night—is the ocean currents, which the Bonaire dive guides warn can take you all the way to Venezuela.

While preparing at our hotel for our first Klein night dive, Susan and I reminisce about our most adventurous night dive. I share this here to give you an idea of some of the challenges involved in getting underwater pictures.

Above: Scorpionfish, Bonaire

This rare juvenile reef scorpionfish is about the size of my thumb. In this flash photograph, the fish's red color makes it easy to see. However, when viewed in natural light, the animal looks almost black, and therefore almost invisible to most fish.

Right: Schoolmaster Snapper, Bonaire

The schoolmaster is a member of the snapper family, which get their name from the snapping sound they make when they're caught. Snappers are nocturnal predators and rest in the branches of soft coral trees or in the nooks and crannies of the reef during the day.

Above: Orange Cup Coral Blooming at Night, Bonaire
Photographed well after the sun has set, the polyps of this colony of orange cup coral on a town pier piling burst with color.

Left: Orange Cup Coral During Daytime, Bonaire
You can dive the same reef at different times of the day and have a completely different visual experience on each dive. During daylight hours, for example, orange cup corals retract their polyps.

Sleeping Filefish, Bonaire
Filefish are often found drifting in or resting on the long branches of gorgonians. They can change color from brown to gray, which helps them to blend in with their surroundings. Like most fish, these are more easily photographed at night when they are sleeping than during the day. They get their name from the sharp "file" on their back, which doesn't feel too good in a predator's mouth.

Above: Scorpionfish, Bonaire
If you were not looking for it, the scorpionfish would be almost impossible to detect. The key to locating hard-to-see fish is to use a dive light, which creates strong shadows that help to outline the animals' bodies. The key to getting good photographs of well-camouflaged fish is to use an underwater strobe.

Left: Trunkfish, Bonaire
Many reef fish swim by moving their bodies while also moving their fins. The hard-bodied trunkfish, however, can only move by propelling itself with its fins, making movement slow and awkward. But with a hard body, the trunkfish has few predators, so having the capability for a quick escape is not necessary for survival.

We were exploring the reefs off the coast of Kenya in 1988. Our dive boat, a rickety wooden Arab dhow, had left the pier at nine at night, and we hoped to be at a dive site by nine-thirty. At ten, we were still cruising in the near total blackness of night. At eleven, we were still cruising. Throughout the journey, the captain of the dhow assured us that he knew where he was going — to the reef that offered the best night dive in Kenya.

Actually, we didn't mind the long delay. The water was calm, and we saw, for the first time, the famed Southern Cross, a dramatic constellation that is not visible in the sky above the equator. We were with great people who shared dive and travel stories, so we soon developed a sense of camaraderie. Around midnight, the captain stopped the engine and dropped anchor. "Gear up," he said. "We're here."

Susan and I entered the tar black water, not knowing how far it would be to the bottom. At a depth of thirty feet (9 m), the reef came into view. Within forty minutes, we had seen five Spanish dancers, one of the most beautiful nudibranchs in the sea and certainly one of the most photographically sought after; a sleeping turtle; dozens of easily photographed, sleeping fish; free-swimming eels; and, the icing on the cake, a cuttlefish, a relative of the squid and the octopus that changes color and shape in an instant.

It was a great night dive indeed. But upon surfacing, about five miles (8 km) from the coast, we did a 360-degree turn — and the dhow was nowhere in sight. We kept looking, and all we saw was darkness. A sense of panic began to set in. Could the underwater currents have taken us so far away from the boat? Could the crew have fallen asleep and drifted away with the surface current? Or could they simply have forgotten that we were in the water and have headed for shore with the other divers on board? These questions raced through our minds.

Getting a grip on ourselves and thinking logically, we did another 360-degree turn, this time with our dive lights on. There, in our beams, about fifty yards (45 m) away, was the hull of the dhow; the crew had turned off all the lights so so they could enjoy the stars. We swam to safety, and then briefed the crew on our safety requirements for night diving.

* * *

Tonight, our dive site, one of twenty-one mooring sites on Klein, is described in the literature as "Just a Nice Dive." Susan and I give each other the OK sign and leap into the midnight sea. The moon is full and there is not a cloud in the sky, so we can see the reef even without the aid of our dive lights.

We drop down to the sandy bottom at about forty feet (12 m). Starfish are on patrol, searching for seashell-dwelling animals (called mollusks) to devour. When they find a desirable meal, such as a clam or an oyster, they cover the shell and, with their strong muscles, slowly and surely pull the shell apart — just far enough so the starfish can insert its stomach into the shell. Then, the starfish secretes digestive enzymes into the shell that dissolve the mollusk so the starfish can ingest it.

If the starfish loses an arm to an eel or to another fish while on patrol, it can generate a new one, which is interesting to scientists who study regeneration of human tissue. What is even more astounding is that some species of starfish can grow an entire new body from a single arm, as long as part of the body is still attached.

Sea cucumbers, the vacuum cleaners of the sea, are also out, sifting through the sand for microorganisms. And there are dozens of long-spined sea urchins, whose sharp, barbed spines can penetrate a diver's wet suit, causing pain for a few days. During our exploration of the sand flats we see a myriad of other marine creatures, including a spiny lobster; a tube anemone; conchs; and, in the turtle grass, several different species of crabs, fish, and nudibranchs. Although they are not as colorful as the coral reef, the sand flats offer divers easy access to many creatures that are essential to maintaining the harmony of the rhythm of the reef.

Having thoroughly explored the sand flats, we move toward the reef. Here, in the countless nooks and crannies, we find fish sleeping, posed for pictures. I always give would-be underwater photographers who want to get great pictures of free-swimming fish the following

Crab, Bonaire
Clinging crabs, like many crustaceans, hide in reefs—artificial and natural—during the day. At night, they leave the safety of their hide-outs and scavenge for food, using their powerful claws to trap small shrimp and other bottom dwellers. Crabs can run forward, backward, and from side to side at a fairly quick pace. When threatened, they raise their claws as a way of saying, "Stay away, or else!"

tip: dive at night. When the fish are in this half-sleep state, they are easy to approach; in the daytime, getting close to free-swimming fish is nearly impossible.

I photograph a snoozing juvenile French angelfish that at this stage of its life has a black body with bold yellow stripes. By the time it is an adult it will have a blue body accented with yellow highlights. Then I see an adult bluehead wrasse, which started life with a yellow and white body but now has a blue head and a blue, black, and white body. Many reef fish change color as they mature, when they change sex, when they are mating, and even throughout the day to avoid detection by predators. Scientists suggest that color change helps other fish of the same species know who is available for mating; it also helps distinguish juvenile cleaner fish from non-cleaner adults of the same species. Learning to identify fish adds to the enjoyment of scuba diving, and I highly recommend the identification guides listed at the back of this book to help you keep track of the fish in their different color phases.

There are other adults sleeping here—butterflyfish, creolefish, and tangs. Like most diurnal fish, they have lost some of the brilliant luster of their daytime color and now look rather drab. Why they fade at night is a puzzle to marine scientists. After all, in the darkness they are almost invisible anyway.

It is time to head back to the boat. I have one exposure left and would like to photograph more sleeping fish, but I have learned from experience that when I have one exposure remaining in my camera, I should save it in case I encounter that totally unique picture opportunity.

There it is, a long-lure frogfish—perhaps the best camouflaged and least photographed creature on the reef. It is resting on an orange sponge, whose color it mimics perfectly. I certainly would not have seen it had it not been for the fish's failed attempt to suck in a passing fish, which I had been following in the beam of my dive light. I make my exposure and head toward the boat with Susan.

Just below the surface, we switch off our dive lights—and we are alone with nature. Looking up, we can clearly see the outline of the full moon. Around us, more bioluminescent algae sparkle like stars. It is a breathtaking sight and an enthralling feeling that really must be experienced to be fully appreciated.

Above: Sea Anemone, Bonaire
Night dives hold many surprises, if you take your time and look for them. The tentacles of this sea anemone hold a world of their own.

Left: Cleaner Shrimp, Bonaire
I spotted this inch-long (2.5-cm) spotted cleaning shrimp hiding among the protective tentacles of a sea anemone. Sometimes I stay in one spot for fifteen minutes in search of interesting marine creatures.

Opposite: Gray Angelfish, Bonaire
Most fish go through dramatic color changes as they grow from juvenile to adult. This juvenile gray angelfish will lose its brilliant yellow stripes as an adult, turning a dull gray with black speckles."

Chapter 6

Changing Rhythm
The Future of the Coral Reef

There is really only one ocean on planet Earth. We have given different areas different names for convenience's sake. What happens on the other side of the planet eventually affects us, and vice versa. — Dr. Ernie Ernst, CEDAM International Advisor

Around the world, in virtually all the oceans, the natural and age-old rhythm and balance of the reef are being upset by human activity. We are destroying some of the most biologically diverse habitats on earth and reducing the number of sea mammals, fish, and invertebrates that depend on each other for survival. Someone once asked me, "What does it matter what happens in Galápagos?" The fact is, as my friend Dr. Ernst points out, there is really only one ocean and we all are connected to and linked by that ocean. What happens thousands of miles away may not immediately affect another area of the world, but if destructive events keep moving closer and closer, a change will certainly be noticeable.

Fishing the Reefs to Death

In many parts of the Indo-Pacific, dynamite fishing is common. Hunters toss a bomb into the water, and the stunned fish float to the surface, where they are scooped up with ease. The loss of fish — including species that have absolutely no commercial value — is bad enough. Added to this rape of the sea is the destruction of the coral reef. Those responsible for this destruction do not seem to realize that someday they will run out of reefs to dynamite. In the Philippines, time is indeed running out — according to marine scientists, bombs have destroyed 75 percent of the reefs.

In many parts of the Atlantic and Pacific, commercial fishing boats use "long lines" — fishing lines up to twenty miles (32 km) long. These lines catch not only tuna and swordfish, but also dolphins and manta rays. Dolphins and rays have no commercial value, and the fishermen toss these dead and dying animals back into the water. On my recent trip to Truk Lagoon in Chuuk,

Jack School, Cocos Island
This dense school of jacks is patrolling the protected waters off Cocos Island. It's an awe-inspiring experience to dive with so many wild animals. Scenes such as this are disappearing in many parts of the world because drift nets, some the size of Manhattan Island, are wiping out fish populations in astonishing numbers.

Above: Dynamite Fishing Effects, Indonesia
As the population of our planet increases, our food sources decrease. In Indonesia, fishermen use dynamite to fish; the dead or stunned fish float to the surface after the explosion. But the explosion also kills the reef and after the fish are gone the entire village moves to another island. Dynamite fishing has damaged 40 percent of the reefs in Indonesia.

Right: Netted Hammerhead Shark, Galápagos Islands
In 1994, more than 100 million sharks were caught and slaughtered for their fins. Shark fins are sold to Asian distributors, who use the fins for shark fin soup, considered a delicacy in many Far Eastern countries. This scalloped hammerhead shark has been caught in an illegally set net off the Galápagos Islands. Photograph © by Doug Perrine

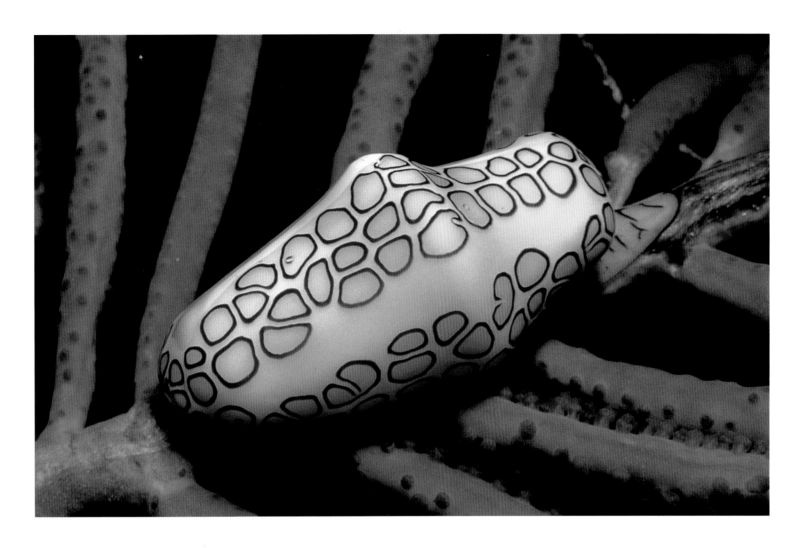

Above: Flamingo Tongue Shell, Belize
This beautiful flamingo tongue shell only looks beautiful when its mantel is exposed, as illustrated. Shell-collecting scuba divers often find this shell in this phase, but are disappointed to find a bland-looking shell once they surface. All shells, pretty or ugly, should be left in the sea, for each species plays an important role in the reef's survival. "Look, don't touch," should be the rule with all scuba divers when exploring the marine environment. Also remember that contact with sponges and corals can damage the animal's outer tissue, which protects it from disease, parasites, and predators.

Left: Sea Urchins, Canouan
Sea urchins, like these West Indian sea eggs, eat algae and other bottom-dwelling organisms. When they are overfished—primarily for their tasty roe—the delicate rhythm of the reef is upset.

Micronesia, the local marine biologist told me that there were ninety long-line fishing boats working in the area. I think it is safe to say that when my three-year-old son Marco dives in Chuuk, the underwater habitat will be totally different from what it is today.

There is more bad news. Drift nets, some the size of Manhattan Island, are used to catch everything that floats and swims in the sea. These massive killing machines wreak havoc on an area by wiping out entire populations of some animals. What is more, many sea birds dive into the nets for an easy catch but wind up being caught themselves.

The aforementioned fishing techniques, along with more conventional methods, result in an annual catch of more than 500,000 tons (455,000 metric tons) of fish. Obviously, this has a negative effect on the marine environment.

Coral Reef Ecosystem Destruction

Along the coastline of some tropical paradises, people are building hotels and resorts. Before construction begins, workers remove mangroves—which are breeding and feeding areas for many reef fish. In some cases, developers dredge lagoons—also important feeding areas—so that boats can easily slip into new harbors.

Underwater bombs are used for a destructive purpose other than fishing. They are an effective, fast, and easy way to blast the reef for building materials. In the Indian and Pacific Oceans, workers mine the reefs and use the hard, weather-resistant limestone to make roads and sidewalks in nearby countries. In Sri Lanka, for instance, many of the roads are made from blasted coral.

Of course, we can't discuss our endangered oceans without mention-

Saving Coral, Key Largo
This diver is not attacking the reef. Rather, she is using wire clippers to remove broken fishing line that has become entangled on the coral. Reef rescuers are growing in numbers, as divers become more and more aware of the fragile marine environment.

ing pollution. Around the world, factories dump waste products into the ocean; human waste and the run-off from agricultural chemicals spill into the sea; and oil spills from damaged ships devastate entire ecosystems. Whether the pollution is intentional or not, it can damage the marine environment for years, perhaps even changing it in some way forever. These are but a few examples of the threats to coral reefs. We should not blame big business for all the reefs' problems, either. We need to take some of the responsibility ourselves.

Commercial Collectors

The practice of collecting tropical fish for aquariums is getting out of hand. In some cases, commercial fish collectors squirt chemicals into the holes in the reef where the fish hide. These chemicals stun the fish, which are then easily caught. It is important to remember that the removal of just one species from a reef can upset the balance of the whole ecosystem.

Consider herbivores, such as damselfish, for example. These small fish actually "farm" sections of algae on the reef. These fish are extremely protective of their algae farms and attack larger fish—and divers—when they feel threatened. If these herbivores disappeared from the reef, the algae would grow out of control and smother sections of coral.

Corals and coral reefs are being harvested for collector and jewelry markets around the world. Some of the prettiest corals, such as hard brain coral and soft sea fans, are used as decorations to add a "sense of the sea" to a living room or play room. Seashells, an important part of the coral reef ecosystem, are also harvested in great numbers to be used as room decorations.

Protecting the Reef, Red Sea
Amateur scuba divers are helping to protect the reefs of the world by joining marine conservation organizations. These divers—Dave and Noreen Downs—are documenting a sea anemone and its resident clownfish in the Red Sea as part of a scientific CEDAM International study on these animals.

Although a shell may appear to be empty, a small animal may be inside; and abandoned shells quickly become homes for other animals such as hermit crabs and octopuses. Then there are the marine creatures—sharks, seahorses, and giant clams, to name a few—that are harvested because people believe products made from these animals increase sexual potency. As any marine scientist will tell you, the power of these substances as aphrodisiacs lies in the mind of the consumer rather than in the products themselves.

I read in a 1994 *National Geographic* article by Canadian zoologist Amanda Vincent that "at least 20 million individuals from the world's roughly 35 species [of seahorses] are captured and processed annually for medicines and aphrodisiacs in Asia and for aquarium exhibits, curios, and delicacies worldwide." As the harvesting continues, the rhythm of the reef continues to change for the worse.

Consequences
What would happen if a yet-to-be discovered coral, sponge, or alga was wiped out? This could be a disaster for a reason many people do not immediately realize. Researchers at the National Cancer

Institute in Bethesda, Maryland, are constantly testing marine plants and animals to see if they contain compounds that may be effective against cancer. These scientists have made significant discoveries, including the 1994 discovery of a toxin in a sponge that can arrest breast cancer. Many scientists feel marine plants and animals hold the cure to many diseases, but research must continue. If species become extinct, it's possible that we may never find the cures for some diseases.

Effective Conservation

That's some of the bad news. The good news is that conservation organizations are making headway in their fight to protect the marine environment. In several Caribbean countries, including Belize, Bonaire, and Costa Rica, governments have established marine parks. Fishing and shell and coral collecting are banned in these protected areas. In the case of Belize's Hol Chan Marine Reserve, formerly a fished-out area, the fish have returned and the corals are healthy. In Costa Rica's Cocos Island Marine Reserve, where fishing is prohibited within a five-mile (8 km) radius of the island, marine scientists are impressed, not only by the numbers of fish but also with the diversity of the species. Dr. Bob Lavenberg, curator of vertebrates at the Los Angeles County Museum, has documented 309 species in his twenty-two years of diving in Cocos. Other examples of successful marine parks are the Galápagos Marine Reserve and the Great Barrier Marine Park in Australia. More and more parks are planned, so there is hope for the future of the coral reefs in those areas.

Global Change

Most people have heard of global warming, but few realize that an increase in the earth's temperature affects coral reefs. The average temperature around the globe is expected to rise 0.54°F (0.3°C) per decade, producing an increase of about 4.5°F (2.5°C) by 2100. Many marine scientists believe that warmer water may cause some hard corals to lose the photosynthesizing algae that help them grow. When hard corals lose their algae, they turn white. This is known as coral bleaching. Juvenile corals seem to depend on algae for growth more than adults do, and corals can live without the algae, but they grow much faster with them. If the bleaching is not severe, bleached corals can regain their algae.

In addition to global warming, scientists predict a rise in sea level in coming years. Although this will not threaten most coral reef ecosystems and may permit upward growth of coral reef flats, it will affect the habitability of low coral islands and coastal areas. According to noted marine scientists Clive R. Wilkinson and Robert W. Buddemeier, who edited a book for the World Conservation Union entitled *Global Climate Change and Coral Reefs: Implications for People and Reefs*, "The threat to human societies [from a rise in sea level] will necessitate urgent international assistance to those affected countries with lands that will be rendered uninhabitable." A rise in sea level will also affect sea turtles, which may lose their nesting sites if water covers the beaches on which they lay their eggs.

Other climate changes that are expected to change the rhythm of the reef include increased rainfall, which means an increase in sediment run-off, and an increase in major storms. Silt and sediment run-off (caused by the removal of mangroves, construction on land, or dredging) can smother coral, which then has little chance of survival. Furthermore, run-off usually lowers the salinity of sea water, which can also kill corals. I have seen cyclone destruction in Tahiti and on the Great Barrier Reef in Australia and can testify to the destructive nature of such storms. Apart from the havoc wreaked by the storms themselves, scientists worry that an increase in major storms may cause a shift in ocean currents that could be destructive to coral reefs.

What You Can Do to Help Save the Reefs

The World Conservation Union suggests there are two major strategies for managing coral reefs in the face of global climate change: "Remove the causes of climate change by alerting the international community to the impact of greenhouse gas emission; and assess the vulnerability and potential impact on coral reefs and islands, and then prepare local and regional mitigation responses."

You can help protect the marine environment in more direct ways, too. Coral bleaching is of great concern to marine biologists and should be reported to either the Marine Ecological Disturbance Information Center, Department of Marine Sciences, University of Puerto Rico, P.O. Box 908, Lajas, Puerto Rico 00667, or

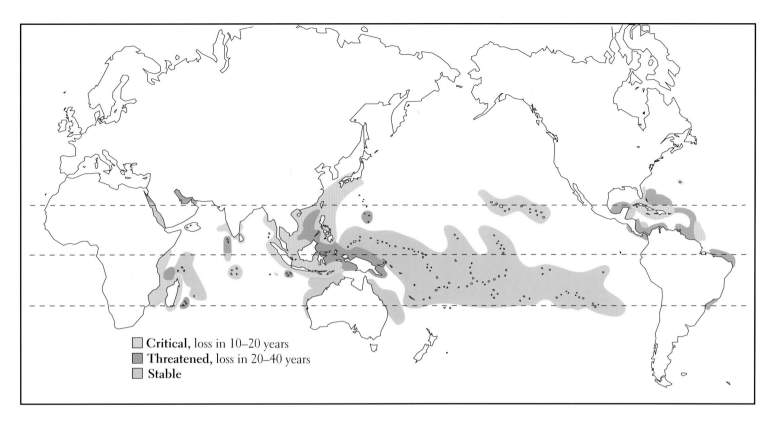

Threatened Coral Reefs

From a conservation standpoint, coral reefs around the world are classified into three categories: critical—reefs under severe stress that will likely collapse within ten to twenty years; threatened—reefs under increasing stress that will collapse within twenty to forty years unless management and conservation efforts are implemented; and stable—reefs remote from population stress or under effective management that should suffer minor impacts within the next one hundred years. Reprinted with permission from Coral Reefs of the World are Facing Widespread Devastation: Can We Prevent This Through Sustainable Management Practices? *by Clive R. Wilkinson.*

Wildlife Conservation, Bronx, New York 10406.

By joining a marine conservation organization, such as Wildlife Conservation, you can either help fund on-going projects or, as a member of a team, assist a scientist on a field expedition. On these field projects, you may be mapping a reef or documenting the number of fish or corals in an area. You will be putting your time under water to good use and helping science at the same time. All you need is the desire to learn and the willingness to be a team player. You will, however, have to pay all your own expenses for the trip.

Finally, if you are a scuba diver or plan to take up this exciting sport, there are things you can do under water to protect the reef.

If you are diving from a small boat and there is no mooring buoy to tie up to, place your anchor carefully in the sand. If you carelessly drop your anchor, you may break off a large section of coral, which may take years to grow back.

Don't touch the corals. If you do, you'll wipe off the protective mucous coating that fights off infection and keeps other corals and algae from overtaking them.

Don't collect shells, beautiful though they may be. You could be collecting a live animal or depriving one of a home.

When diving, remember the diver's creed: Take only pictures, leave only bubbles.

Appendix 1

Reef Conservation Around the World

I have given you an idea of what it is like to dive coral reefs. If you would like to try it for yourself, here is a list of coral reef dive sites around the world where conservation efforts are in effect to protect the reefs. If a site sounds good to you, my suggestion is to research it completely before you go to find out about factors like weather, visibility, accommodation, and marine life. Scuba diving magazines such as *Rodale's Scuba Diving* accurately report on dive destinations.

Different divers like different underwater attractions. Some like swimming with big pelagics, such as whale sharks and manta rays; others like exploring coral kingdoms with their intricate coral castles, exotic tropical fish, and alienlike vertebrates. Although each underwater habitat shares creatures, colors, and corals with other reefs in a rhythm that is common throughout the oceans, each reef also has its own distinctive signature—a characteristic that makes it "something special" to scuba divers. I hope conservation efforts now and in the future will make it possible for future generations of divers to seek out their own special places in coral reef ecosystems around the world.

Bahamas

The northern coral reefs of the Bahamas host a limited number and variety of corals and fish. What you will find in the clear waters of the Bahamas, however, are dive operators who will take you out diving with sharks and dolphins.

At UNEXSO (the Underwater Explorers Society) on Grand Bahama, you can scuba dive with Atlantic bottle-nosed dolphins and Caribbean reef sharks, which have been hand fed by trainers and have become accustomed to divers. Swimming in open water with dolphins is a real treat, and to have sharks swim just inches over your head is a thrill—for some. Whether you've "been there, done that" or just want to get close to some of the largest animals in the sea, you can't beat shark and dolphin encounters.

As a conservationist, I normally am against feeding sharks and dolphins. However, UNEXSO spends about $250,000 a year on fresh fish so their animals stay healthy, whereas they could spend under $50,000 for low-quality fish. Also, UNEXSO has very strict rules about diving with the animals, which keeps cowboy divers under control.

Cenote, Yucatan Peninsula, Mexico
"We are the first generation to explore the underwater environment. Let's hope we are not the last."
—George Page, host of PBS's Nature.

Belize Barrier Reef, Central America

Running from the tip of Mexico's Yucatan Peninsula south to the Gulf of Honduras, the Belize Barrier Reef is one of the largest reef systems in the world, second only to Australia's Great Barrier Reef.

Near shore, divers can explore the mangroves, lagoon, and reef that make up this ecosystem. Off shore, divers find untouched and breathtaking coral reefs on Glovers Reef and Lighthouse Reef—atolls that offer both shallow-water and deep-water reef explorations. For adventure dives in the Caribbean, Belize can't be beat.

For conservationists, Belize is a living laboratory. In 1987, the Hol Chan Marine Reserve was established on Ambergris Cay. This was the first marine preserve in Belize and has illustrated—to fishermen, government officials, tourist operators, and conservationists—that conservation does indeed work if we implement a manageable plan.

Cayman Islands, Caribbean

Cayman is one of the more popular dive destinations in the Caribbean. It's located just south of Cuba, so you can be there in under three hours from Miami.

Grand Cayman is very civilized. You can stay in an air-conditioned Hyatt, have room service, and drive around on good roads. The reefs of Grand Cayman show the effects of heavy diving traffic and construction run-off from the shore; however, you will have a unique experience at Sting Ray City, where, in twelve feet (3.6 m) of water, dozens of tame and harmless sting rays can be hand fed.

In my opinion, the best reef diving in the Caymans is on Bloody Bay Wall off the lee side of Little Cayman, where you can stay in non–air-conditioned huts and go barefoot to dinner. My style, any day, for sure. Because the Ministry of Natural Resources protects the marine environment, and because dedicated park rangers patrol the area, the reefs of Cayman should stay healthy for many years to come.

Fiji, South Pacific

All underwater dive destinations have a trademark that makes each site unique. In the Fiji Islands, situated about 2,500 miles (4,000 km) east of Australia's Great Barrier Reef, the draw is soft corals in colors that add incomparable beauty to the untouched, pristine reefs. These brilliantly colored soft corals make the two-day trip from the West Coast of the United States worth the effort. Once you are under water in Fiji, you will be simply overwhelmed by the sights you will see.

If you make it to Fiji, I urge you to visit a Fijian village. The people here are very friendly, and if you are lucky, the Fijians may even invite you for a meal, some dancing, and a drink or two of kava—a local drink that tastes like mud and, some say, makes one feel slightly intoxicated. I had five cups and didn't feel a thing, but I was relaxed and had a great time—until my traditional Fijian wraparound skirt, or sulu, fell off while I was dancing with three Fijian girls. When you go to Fiji, you need to get permission from a chief to dive in his tribe's waters and to assure him that you will not damage the reef.

Galápagos Islands, Ecuador

In 1835, celebrated naturalist Charles Darwin visited the Galápagos archipelago, located about six hundred miles (960 km) off the coast of Ecuador. Today, Galápagos offers divers the thrill of a lifetime—diving with friendly sea lions. I've been to Galápagos twice, and on virtually every dive, several playful sea lions have been my diving buddies, swimming around underwater as gracefully as ballerinas move across a stage. Whale sharks—some as long as a school bus, hammerhead sharks, and schools of large fish are also attractions. On a smaller scale, you'll find a wide variety of fish, but don't expect to see much coral. The water is a just a bit too cool for coral reefs to thrive.

When I began writing this book in 1994, shark fishing was out of control in Galápagos, as were grouper fishing and sea cucumber harvesting—even though the waters surrounding Galápagos are officially protected by the Galápagos Marine Park Authority. If overfishing like this had continued, it would have upset the entire ecosystem of Galápagos, and ruined the rhythm of these reefs forever. The good news is that, in 1994, with urging from several local conservationists, as well as the Galápagos Marine Park Authority and international conservation groups, the president of Galápagos signed a marine conservation law that banned fishing within a forty-mile (64-km) radius of the islands.

Great Barrier Reef, Australia

The Great Barrier Reef, located off Australia's northeast coast, is actually a series of small ribbon reefs that form one huge reef system—the largest in the world. And what a system it is! Here, underwater explorers can find hundreds of species of corals and fish—from one-inch-long (2.5-cm) gobies to great white sharks that reach lengths of thirteen feet (3.9 m) or more.

Don't let the threat of the great white scare you off, however. Most great whites are found in the cooler waters of southern Australia, and even there sightings of these hunters are few and far between. To attract a great white shark—which, believe it or not, some divers want to see under water while protected in a special shark cage—tour operators have to "chum" the water with blood, dead chickens, and fish heads for hours, even days, at a time. Then, if they are lucky, they may find a great white.

Box jellyfish, blue-ringed octopuses, and sea snakes—all of which can be deadly—pose greater threats to divers than do the sharks. But if you are careful and dive with an experienced tour operator, you shouldn't have a problem while exploring this underwater wonderland.

The Great Barrier Reef is managed by the Great Barrier Reef Marine Park Authority, which has developed a conservation plan that keeps the reefs healthy while allowing some commercial fishing. It is a plan other marine parks around the world could use as a basis for their own programs.

Kenya, East Africa

Kenya is world famous for its terrestrial wildlife. Just about everyone has seen East African safaris on television. An underwater safari on the Kenyan coast offers a different perspective on the diversity of life in this part of the world. I found the reefs of Kenya to be similar to those of the Red Sea: colorful soft corals teeming with small reef fish. In some areas, I encountered hard coral gardens that stretched as far as the eye could see—about one hundred feet (30 m).

Conservation in Kenya is becoming more important, as the Kenyan government realizes the importance of protecting natural resources that generate valuable tourist dollars every year. Marine parks have been established and funding is coming, although, like all things in Africa, it is coming slowly.

Key Largo, Florida

I first dived in Key Largo in 1981 and I still enjoy the diving here. For me, it is some of the easiest diving in the world. I can leave Miami at seven in the morning, drive south for about an hour, sign up for a dive at a Key Largo dive shop at eight, and be on the reef by ten. Or, you can stay in a Key Largo hotel and make five dives a day.

The reefs here are not as spectacular as those in Cayman, Belize, or Bonaire because the Keys are at the northern tip of where corals form reefs. However, you may actually encounter more fish if you dive in Key Largo National Marine Sanctuary, which is protected by strict conservation laws that rangers enforce. Key Largo also offers good wreck diving. Some, such as the Civil War wreck, are as shallow as thirty feet (9 m), which is a good depth for novice divers; others, including the *Dwayne* and the *Bibb*, are for more experienced divers and lie in ninety feet (27 m) of water.

CEDAM International advisor John Halas, who is the resource manager for the Florida Keys National Marine Sanctuary, Upper Keys Office, notes that there are probably more fish in the Florida Keys than in some Caribbean islands because of the five- to six-mile (8–10-km) shelf that lies between the land and the reefs. "This shelf is a tremendous nursery for the reef fish," he said, "and it is this area that plays a very important role in the rhythm of the reef in the Florida Keys."

Palau, Micronesia

Palau (called Belau by the people who live there) lies in the middle of an imaginary triangle formed by the Philippines, New Guinea, and Guam. Even with this geographical guideline, the tiny country is hard to find on the map. Luckily, this beautiful tropical island archipelago is easily accessible by Continental Airlines via Guam, and when you get there you'll be amazed at the diversity of marine life. Dr. Robert E. Johannes, among other noted marine scientists, has called Palau the "cradle of diversity" because of the great variety of corals, fish, and algae that thrive here.

Palau also offers a great diversity of scuba diving experiences: drift dives in strong underwater currents sweep divers past schools of sharks and other pelagic fish; cave dives offer underwater explorations into the mysterious world of stalactites and stalagmites; near-vertical wall dives let scuba divers see how the structure of the reef changes as depth increases and light decreases; and shallow coral gardens allow snorkelers to get a look at the fascinating world of the coral reef.

At CEDAM International's 1989 Seven Underwater Wonders of the World meeting, scientists rated this site as the number-one underwater wonder of the world. Today, the reefs of Palau are healthy and pristine, in part because the government has strict conservation laws that ban dynamite fishing and that limit other kinds of fishing and coastal development.

Seychelles, Indian Ocean

About 1,500 miles (2,400 km) off the coast of Kenya, you will find some of the most beautiful islands in the world: the Seychelles. In all my travels, I'd say that the Seychelles have the finest, whitest beaches I have ever seen.

These are the only beaches in the world where the hawksbill turtles make their nests during daylight hours. Once on the beach, poachers slaughter many turtles for their shells, which are used for jewelry; and for their meat, which is considered a delicacy. Turtle harvesting is illegal, but there are not enough rangers to patrol all the islands. Under water, you will not find typical tropical coral reefs, because the smooth granite shoals make it hard for corals to gain a strong foothold; however, you will find many Indo-Pacific fish and several species of hard and soft corals.

There are four marine parks in the Seychelles, and park rangers patrol these areas to ensure that no shell or coral collecting and no fishing or polluting activities occur. The Seychelles marine parks are administered by the Seychelles National Environment Commission, which monitors both the marine and terrestrial reserves.

Marine Conservation Organizations You Can Join

CEDAM International
One Fox Road
Croton-on-Hudson, NY 10520
USA

Center for Marine Conservation
1725 DeSales Street NW
Washington, D.C. 20036 USA

Centro Ecologico Akumal
A.C.
Apartado Postal #127
Playa del Carman
Q. Roo, Mexico 77710

Coral Cay Conservation Ltd.
The Sutton Business Centre
Restmore Way
Wallington, Surrey SM6 7AH
United Kingdom

Cousteau Society
8440 Santa Monica Boulevard
Los Angeles, CA 90069 USA

EarthWatch
680 Mount Auburn Street
Watertown, MA 02272 USA

Global Coral Reef Alliance
324 North Bedford Road
Chappaqua, NY 10514 USA

Ocean Voice International, Inc.
2883 Otterson Drive
Ottawa, ON K1V 7B2
Canada

Pronature
Apartado Postal #64
C.A.P. Dante
97100 Merida
Yucatan, Mexico

ReefWatch
Tropical Marine Research Unit
Department of Biology
University of York
York Y01 5DD
United Kingdom

Wildlife Conservation
Bronx Zoo
Bronx, NY 10460 USA

World Wildlife Fund–Australia
Level 17, St. Martins Tower
31 Market Street, GPO 528
Sydney, New South Wales
2001
Australia

Appendix 2

Photography Beneath the Waves

When I go on a dive trip, I pack in my dive bag mask, snorkel, fins, booties, wet suit, regulator, depth gauge, diving computer, pressure gauge, buoyancy compensator, weight belt, and extra fin and mask straps. On site, I rent a tank and weights.

I send my dive bag through baggage. If it is lost or delayed, I can rent scuba gear, though it may not be exactly what I am used to. I hand-carry all my cameras—I can't take the chance of not having my time-proven photographic equipment on site when I arrive. In some locations I could rent or buy gear; however, because even new cameras may be slightly "off" when it comes to exposures, I would have to shoot several test rolls to fine-tune the new equipment.

Getting my underwater camera system to fit in two carry-on bags is a challenge. Here's what I usually take: two Nikonos V camera bodies, two 15mm lenses, one 20mm lens, viewfinders for the 15mm and 20mm lenses, a 35mm lens with extension tubes, two Nikonos SB–103 strobes, one Sea & Sea YS–300 strobe, a Canon underwater housing, a Canon EOS A2E, a Canon 60mm lens, a Canon 20mm lens, a wide-angle dome port and a macro flat port for the housing, several flash sync cords, a mini-tool kit, and as many batteries and as much film as I can fit in between all the gear. I also pack extra film and batteries in my dive bag.

I have two favorite carry-on bags, one with built-in wheels that fits down the aisle on the plane and into the overhead compartment on most jets, and one over-the-shoulder bag that I fit under the seat in front of me.

Why do I take so much stuff? Because, inevitably, one piece of equipment will flood, and I'll need back-up gear. Also, I often dive with two cameras, one for macro and one for wide-angle photography, while my assistant carries a camera or two. Under water, where time is strictly limited, you must be prepared for every encounter and opportunity.

You don't need all this gear to get great photos, however. With an automatic Sea & Sea Motor Marine IIEX, Sea & Sea accessory strobe, and ISO 400 color print film, you can get good results your first time out—or under.

Photo Tips

Shooting on automatic will give you a high percentage of properly exposed pictures.

Fill the frame with the subject.

Don't take pictures of subjects that are more than six feet (2 m) away.

Think of taking a few great shots, which may require waiting for the correct light or most interesting subject, rather than lots of snapshots.

If you'd like more information on underwater photography, check out another one of my Voyageur Press books, *The Complete Guide to Photographing Underwater Wonders*. In this take-any-where book you'll find easy-to-use information on capturing on film the beauty of the underwater environment.

Suggested Reading

Reading is one of the keys to knowledge, and knowledge is the key to understanding the secrets of the sea. It was by reading every book I could find on the marine environment that I learned much of what I know about life beneath the waves. If you want to increase your knowledge of and appreciation for the fascinating fish, corals, and other invertebrates of the world's coral reefs, check out these books, which are some of the best I've seen.

Auerbach, Paul S. *A Medical Guide to Hazardous Marine Life*. Jacksonville, FL: Progressive Printing, 1987.

Banister, Keith and Andrew Campbell. *Encyclopedia of Aquatic Life*. New York: Facts on File, 1985.

Cohne, Shlomo. *Red Sea Diver's Guide*. Tel Aviv, Israel: SEAPEN, 1991.

Faulkner, Douglas and Richard Chesher. *Living Corals*. New York, NY: Crown, 1979.

Fautin, Daphne and Gerald Allen. *Field Guide to Anemonefish and Their Host Anemones*. Perth, Australia: Western Australia Museum, 1992.

Greenpeace Book of Coral Reefs. New York: Sterling, 1992.

Fowler, Jim. *Jim Fowler's Wildest Places on Earth*. Richmond, VA: Time-Life Custom Publishing, 1994.

Halas, John and Judy Halas. *Diving and Snorkeling Guide to the Florida Keys*. Houston, TX: Pisces Books, 1987.

Humann, Paul. *Coral Identification*. Jacksonville, FL: New World Publications, 1993.

Humann, Paul. *Reef Creature Identification*. Jacksonville, FL: New World Publications, 1993.

Clownfish, Red Sea

Taking underwater pictures is fun. However, it's also lots of hard work. You need good photographic technique and equipment, good diving skills, an understanding of what you are looking at through your camera's viewfinder, an interesting subject, and—equally as important as the aforementioned qualities—luck. I photographed these clownfish with an SLR in an underwater housing. I used a 20mm lens, which provided good depth of field, and one strobe, which brought out the true color of the subjects.

Humann, Paul. *Reef Fish Identification*. Jacksonville, FL: New World Publications, 1993.

Humann, Paul. *Reef Fish Identification: Galápagos*. Jacksonville, FL: New World Publications, 1994.

Lewbel, George and Larry Marti. *Diving Bonaire*. Locust Valley, NY: Aqua Quest, 1991.

Meyer, Franz. *Diving and Snorkeling Guide to Belize*. Houston, TX: Pisces Books, 1990.

Ocean Facts. Tulsa, OK: EDC Publishing, 1992.

Rock, Tim. *Diving and Snorkeling Guide to Truk Lagoon*. Houston, TX: Pisces Books, 1994.

Wilson, Roberta and James Wilson. *Watching Fishes*. Houston, TX: Pisces Books, 1992.

If you are concerned about the changing rhythm of the world's reefs and would like to learn more about the problems they face, the following two publications published by The World Conservation Union will be of great interest:

Global Climate Change and Coral Reefs: Implications for People and Reefs. Cambridge, MA: IUCN, n.d.

Reefs at Risk. Cambridge, MA: IUCN, n.d.

For information and pictures of my own that complement *Rhythm of the Reef*, you may want to read one of my earlier works:

Sammon, Rick. *Seven Underwater Wonders of the World*. Charlottesville, VA: Thomasson-Grant, 1991.

Sammon, Rick. *The Complete Guide to Photographing Underwater Wonders*. Stillwater, MN: Voyageur Press, 1995.

These two books of mine are for children who want to know more about the underwater world:

Sammon, Rick. *Hide and Seek Under the Sea*. Stillwater, MN: Voyageur Press, 1995.

Sammon, Rick and Susan Sammon. *Under the Sea in 3-D*. San Francisco, CA: The Nature Company, 1993.

Index

About the Author

Rick Sammon is the author of twenty-three books and the host of *Digital Photography Workshop* on the Do It Yourself network and guest host of *Photo Safari* on the Outdoor Life Network. He has been published in virtually every photography magazine and many nature magazines, including *National Geographic*, *Wildlife Conservation*, and *National Wildlife*. He is a member of the Explorers Club and president of CEDAM International, which is dedicated to conservation, education, diving, and marine research. Rick has traveled the world with marine scientists in search of elusive marine creatures, leading expeditions to Lake Baikal in Siberia, Fiji, the Red Sea, Venezuela, Honduras, Australia, Belize, Mexico, and Galapagos.

Rick and Susan Sammon *(Photo by Angela Anderson)*